Dear Monica,

May you enjoy many different hors d'ouvres and "countless" cocktail parties using this book. You are already a wonderful cook, let this help you become the "Martha of the Midwest". Happy 37!

All my love &
bon Appetit!
Patty

HORS D'OEUVRES

HORS D'OEUVRES

Eric Treuille and Victoria Blashford-Snell

PHOTOGRAPHY BY IAN O'LEARY

DK Publishing Inc. New York

DK www.dk.com

A D K Publishing, Inc Book

DK www.dk.com

EDITORIAL CONSULTANT Rosie Kindersley
DESIGN AND ART DIRECTION Stuart Jackman
PROJECT EDITOR Julia Pemberton Hellums
US EDITOR Barbara Minton
ASSISTANT EDITOR Sally Somers
PRODUCTION CONTROLLER Elisabeth Cherry

FOOD STYLING Eric Treuille

DEDICATION
To my wife.
To my husband.

First American Edition, 1999
2 4 6 8 10 9 7 5 3 1

Published in the United States by
DK Publishing, Inc.
95 Madison Avenue, New York, New York 10016

Library of Congress Cataloging-in-Publication Data
Treuille, Eric
Hors D'Oeuvres/by Eric Treuille and Victoria Blashford-Snell.
p. cm.
ISBN 0-7894-4895-5 (alk. paper)
1. Appetizers. I Blashford-Snell, Victoria. II Title.
TX740.T72 1999
641.8'12-dc21   99-28960 CIP

Color reproduction in the United Kingdom by DOT Gradations
Printed in Italy by A. Mondadori Editore, Verona

CONTENTS

INTRODUCTION

From the simplest to the grandest party, entertaining means sharing. Since time immemorial, the traditional way to express friendship has been with an open house, a warm welcome, and good food lovingly prepared. We were fortunate enough to grow up in households where home cooked meals were a pleasurable ritual that punctuated our lives. Then, we learned the joy of connecting with family and friends over food. Now, many people don't seem to have the time or the energy to cook, let alone entertain, at home. The constraints of modern life call for a new approach to entertaining. "Can I make that ahead?" is the question we are most often asked at the cooking classes we teach.

An hors d'oeuvres party is a practical way for both experienced and beginner cooks to entertain at home. A large number of guests can be accommodated without matching dinner service, tables, or even chairs. Stacks of dirty pans, dishes, and cutlery cluttering up the sink are not a burden, because hors d'oeuvres are easily hand held with only a small paper napkin and simply eaten. There's no need to worry about spending all day or all night in the kitchen. Canapés are flexible foods that be prepared well ahead of time.

We set out to create a cook book that puts the pleasure back into entertaining. We have included practical tips, techniques, and timing that we hope will inspire you to invite your friends and family to celebrate.

We don't want to turn home cooks into professional caterers. We want to help home cooks be confident cooks, because confident cooks make happy hosts, and happy hosts give great parties.

So, relax. Because everybody loves a party, and home cooked food always makes an occasion special.

Eric Aurora

Notes From the Cooks

BEFORE YOU START read through the recipe carefully. Make sure you have all the equipment and the ingredients required.

On Measuring

Accurate measurements are essential if you want the same good results each time you make a recipe. We have given measurements in non-metric and metric form in all the recipes. Always stick to one set of measurements; never use a mixture of both in the same recipe.

A kitchen scale is the most accurate way to measure dry ingredients. We recommend using scales for all except the smallest amounts.

We recommend using measuring spoons when following a recipe. All spoon measurements in the book are level unless otherwise stated. To measure dry ingredients with a spoon, scoop the ingredient lightly from the storage container, then level the surface with the edge of a straight-bladed knife.

We use standard level spoon measurements
1 tbsp - (15ml)
1 tsp - (5ml)

For maximum accuracy when using graduated measuring cups for dry ingredients, spoon the ingredient loosely into the required cup, mounding it up slightly; then level the surface with the edge of a straight-bladed knife. Do not use the cup as a scoop, pack the ingredient into the cup, or tap the cup on the work surface. This will give you an inaccurate result.

To measure liquids, choose a transparent glass or plastic measuring cup. Always place the cup on a flat surface and check for accuracy at eye level when pouring in a liquid to measure.

A final and important rule of measuring - never measure ingredients over the mixing bowl!

On Oven Temperatures

Always preheat your oven for 10–20 minutes before you will need to use it. This allows it to reach the required temperature. Bear in mind that the higher the temperature required, the longer it will take to preheat the oven.

Ovens vary from kitchen to kitchen. Most have hot spots, so be prepared to rotate dishes from top to bottom or from front to back during the cooking time. A good oven thermometer is an important piece of kitchen equipment.

If using a fan-assisted oven, follow the manufacturer's instructions for adjusting cooking timings and oven temperatures.

On Quantities

However accurately we measure, cooking remains to some extent an unpredictable science. Ingredients vary, so use the yields we give for each recipe as general guidelines. Hors D'oeuvres are bite-size morsels that should be eaten in one mouthful, so be prepared to modify the number of items the recipe yields to suit this criteria. We have done our best to make sure that none of the recipes yield less than the quantity stated, but in some cases a recipe might make a few extra, which will of course allow for both breakage - and tasting!

On Tasting

Always taste food as you cook and before serving it. Don't be afraid to add or change flavors to suit your palate - what's fun about cooking is experimenting, improvising, creating. Ingredients differ from day to day, season to season, kitchen to kitchen; our tomato may be a little riper than your tomato, and so on. Be prepared to the adjust sweetness, sharpness, spiciness, and, most important of all, salt to your own taste.

READY MADE FOR GETTING AHEAD

1 Mayonnaise
2 Bouchée cases
3 Chocolate cups
4 Croustades
5 Filo pastry
6 Hollandaise
7 Puff pastry
8 Pesto
9 Pastry cases
10 Flour tortillas

FINE FOODS FOR SPECIAL OCCASIONS

1. Parmesan cheese
2. Stilton cheese
3. Roquefort cheese
4. Quail eggs
5. Lobster
6. Black lumpfish roe
7. Red lumpfish roe
8. Salmon roe
9. Caviar
10. Medium shrimp
11. Tiger shrimp
12. Bay scallops
13. Sea scallops
14. Crab claw
15. Smoked salmon
16. Proscuitto
17. Oyster

BOLD FLAVORS FOR BITE-SIZED MORSELS

1. Lemon, lime, and orange peel
2. Thai sweet chili sauce
3. Chinese hot chili sauce
4. Tabasco
5. Balsamic vinegar
6. Worcestershire sauce
7. Curry powder
8. Paprika
9. Crushed chili flakes
10. Cayenne
11. Sesame seeds
12. Pickled ginger
13. Horseradish sauce
14. Olives
15. Anchovy fillets
16. Chipotes in adobo
17. Grainy mustard
18. Mustard powder
19. Dijon mustard
20. Chili peppers
21. Fresh herbs
22. Baby capers
23. Capers

KITCHEN TOOLS

1. 2.5cm (1in) fluted pastry cutter
2. 5cm (2in) fluted pastry cutter
3. 4.5cm (1¾in) fluted pastry cutter
4. 6.5cm (2¾in) plain pastry cutter
5. 5cm (2in) plain pastry cutter
6. 3.5cm (1½in) plain pastry cutter
7. 6cm (2½in) star shaped pastry cutter
8. 6cm (2½in) heart shaped cutter

9. 3.5cm (1½in) heart shaped pastry cutter
10. Vegetable peeler
11. Oyster knife
12. Melon baller
13. Zester
14. Olive pitter
15. Serrated knife
16. Chef's knife
17. Kitchen scissors
18. Large star piping nozzle
19. Large plain piping nozzle

BAKEWARE

1. Plain tartlet tin
2. Baking sheet
3. Mini muffin tins
4. Fluted tartlet tins
5. Oven tray

THE RECIPES

READ THROUGH THE RECIPE FIRST.

USE FRESH SEASONAL INGREDIENTS.

HAVE FUN – YOU'RE COOKING FOR A PARTY.

NIBBLES, DIPS, AND DIPPERS

SPICED PARTY NUTS

MAKES 2 CUPS (500ml)

2 cups (250g) blanched almonds
1 tbsp egg white, about ½ an egg white
2 tsp dark brown sugar
2 tsp salt
½ tsp cayenne pepper
1 tbsp finely chopped rosemary

Preheat oven to 300°F (150°C). Spread nuts in a single layer on a baking sheet. Roast, shaking the pan occasionally, until lightly golden, 15 minutes. Remove from oven and cool slightly. Beat egg white until frothy and add nuts, sugar, salt, cayenne, and rosemary. Toss ingredients together to coat each nut well. Return nuts to the oven. Roast until fragrant and golden, 20 minutes. Cool. Serve at room temperature.

THINK AHEAD
Make up to 3 days in advance. Cool and store in an airtight container at room temperature. Alternatively, freeze up to 1 month in advance (see page 149). Defrost overnight in refrigerator. Crisp in a preheated 350°F (180°C) oven, 3 minutes.

COOKS' NOTE
To make curried almonds omit sugar, cayenne, and rosemary and replace with 1tbsp curry powder.

CRUNCHY SWEET AND SPICY PECANS

MAKES 2 CUPS (500ml)

8oz (250g) pecans
1 tbsp sunflower oil
4 tbsp sugar
1 tsp salt
1½ tsp chili powder

Preheat oven to 300°F (150°C). Spread pecans on a baking sheet. Roast, shaking the pan occasionally, until nutty and toasted, 30 minutes. Heat the oil in a frying pan over a medium heat. Add nuts and stir to coat. Sprinkle with sugar and salt. Cook, stirring constantly, until the sugar melts and starts to brown slightly, 5 minutes. Remove from heat but continue stirring until nuts have cooled slightly. Sprinkle over chili powder and toss to coat each nut well. Serve at room temperature.

THINK AHEAD
Make up to 3 days in advance. Cool and store in an airtight container at room temperature. Alternatively, freeze up to 1 month in advance (see page 149). Defrost overnight in refrigerator. Crisp in a preheated 350°F (180°C) oven, 3 minutes.

COOKS' NOTE
Use the variety of chili powders now available at gourmet food shops to achieve slightly different flavors. Ancho chili powder will add a hint of smoky flavor to this piquant mixture.

MEDITERRANEAN MARINATED OLIVES

MAKES 2 CUPS (500ml)

2 cups (250g) black or green olives or a mixture
1 tsp fennel seeds
½ tsp cumin seeds
grated peel of ½ orange
grated peel of ½ lemon
2 garlic cloves, finely chopped
2 tsp crushed chili flakes
1 tsp dried oregano
1 tbsp lemon juice
1 tbsp red wine vinegar
2 tbsp olive oil
1 tbsp finely chopped parsley

If desired, pit olives. Toast fennel and cumin seeds in an ungreased skillet over a low heat until aromatic, 2 minutes. Combine seeds, olives, peels, garlic, chili, oregano, lemon, vinegar, and oil and toss to coat each olive well. Place in an airtight container. Marinate the mixture at room temperature for 8 hours. Shake the container occasionally to remix the ingredients while marinating. Stir in the parsley. Serve at room temperature.

THINK AHEAD
Make up to 1 week in advance, omitting the parsley. Store in an airtight container and refrigerate. Add parsley up to 3 hours before serving.

COOKS' NOTE
Warming the olives will intensify the flavors. Gently heat the marinated olives over a low heat until warmed through, 5 minutes. Serve warm.

SWISS CHEESE ALLUMETTES

MAKES 30
⅞ cup (125g) all-purpose flour
6 tbsp (90g) cold butter, diced
1 egg yolk
4oz (125g) gruyère cheese, grated
salt, black pepper, cayenne pepper
1 egg beaten with 1 tbsp water
1 tbsp grated parmesan cheese

ESSENTIAL EQUIPMENT
baking parchment

Place flour, butter, egg yolk, and cheese, with a pinch each of salt, pepper, and cayenne in a food processor; pulse until the mixture forms a firm pastry. Turn out and knead lightly by hand until smooth.
Roll out pastry on a floured surface to a ¼in (0.5cm) thickness. Cut into strips about ½in (1cm) wide and 3in (7cm) long. Place ¾in (2cm) apart on baking parchment lined baking sheets. Refrigerate until firm, 30 minutes.
Preheat oven to 350°F (180°C).
Brush with beaten egg. Sprinkle with parmesan. Bake until golden brown, 15 minutes. Cool on a wire rack.
Serve warm or at room temperature, with or without dips.

THINK AHEAD
Make allumettes up to 2 weeks in advance. Store in an airtight container at room temperature. Alternatively, make and freeze up to 1 month in advance (see page 149). Defrost and crisp for 3 minutes in preheated 400°F (200°C) oven.

SAVORY SABLES

MAKES 40

1¾ cups (250g) all-purpose flour	¼ tsp dry mustard
1½ cups (175g) cold butter, diced	1 egg yolk beaten with
½lb (250g) gruyère cheese	1 tbsp water
¼ tsp cayenne pepper	

ESSENTIAL EQUIPMENT
2½in (6cm) star shaped pastry cutter, 2½in (6cm) heart shaped pastry cutter, baking parchment

Place flour, butter, cheese, cayenne, and dry mustard in a food processor; pulse until the mixture forms a pastry. Add a little cold water (1 tsp at a time) if necessary to form a ball.
Roll out pastry on a floured surface to a ¼in (0.5cm) thickness. Cut out into decorative shapes with pastry cutters. Place ¾in (2cm) apart on 2 baking parchment lined baking sheets. Refrigerate cut pastry shapes until firm, 30 minutes.
Preheat oven to 350°F (180°C).
Bake until golden brown, 10 minutes. Cool on a wire rack.
Serve warm or at room temperature, with or without dips.

THINK AHEAD
Make sablés up to 2 weeks in advance. Store in an airtight container at room temperature. Alternatively, make and freeze up to 1 month in advance (see page 149). Defrost and crisp for 3 minutes in preheated 200°C (400°F) Gas 6 oven.

FLAVORED SABLE VARIATIONS

SPICY SABLES
Place 2 tsp paprika with the other dry ingredients in the food processor.

SEEDED SABLES
Omit dry mustard . Place 2 tsp caraway seeds with the other dry ingredients in the food processor.

HERBED SABLES
Omit dry mustard . Place 2 tsp finely chopped rosemary with the other dry ingredients in the food processor.

ROQUEFORT SABLES
Omit dry mustard and cayenne. Use a combination of 4oz (125g) crumbled roquefort cheese and 4oz (125g) grated gruyère instead of ½lb (250g) grated gruyère.

PARMESAN AND PINE NUT BISCOTTINI WITH GREEN OLIVES

MAKES 50

¾ cups (100g) pine nuts
1¾ cups (250g) all-purpose flour
1 tsp baking powder
1 tsp salt
¼ tsp black pepper
1 tbsp fennel seeds
2 tbsp grated parmesan cheese
¾ cups(100g) pitted green olives, finely chopped
3 eggs, beaten

Preheat oven to 350°F (180°C). Spread pine nuts in a single layer on a baking sheet. Toast in oven until nutty and golden, 7 minutes. Cool.
Sift flour, baking powder, and salt into a bowl. Add pepper, fennel seeds, parmesan, olives, and eggs and mix with a fork to form a rough dough. Alternatively, place flour, baking powder, salt, pepper, fennel seeds, parmesan, olives, and eggs in a food processor; pulse to a rough dough. Knead the pine nuts into the dough with hands. Divide dough into 4 equal-sized pieces. Shape each piece into a log, 1in (2.5cm) thick and 12in (30cm) long. Place each log on a floured baking sheet. Bake until firm to the touch, 25 minutes. Remove and leave until cool enough to handle. With a serrated knife, cut each biscotti log on the diagonal into ½in (1cm) thick slices. Place the slices in a single layer on the baking sheets. Bake until crisp and dry, 15 minutes. Cool completely on a wire rack.

THINK AHEAD
Make up to 2 weeks in advance. Store in an airtight container at room temperature. Alternatively, freeze the unbaked biscotti logs up to 1 month in advance (see page 149). Defrost overnight in the refrigerator before baking.

TRIPLE CHOCOLATE BISCOTTINI WITH HAZELNUTS

MAKES 50

1⅔ cups (200g) all-purpose flour
1/2 cup (60g) cocoa powder
¾ tsp baking powder
¼ tsp salt
½ cup (150g) sugar

2oz (60g) bittersweet chocolate, chopped
3 eggs, beaten
1 tsp vanilla extract
1 cup (100g) hazelnuts, blanched (see page 163)
3½oz (100g) white chocolate to garnish

ESSENTIAL EQUIPMENT
paper piping bag (see page 146)

Preheat oven 350°F (180°C).
Sift flour, cocoa, baking powder, and salt into a bowl. Add sugar, chocolate, eggs, and vanilla and mix with a fork to form a rough dough. Alternatively, place flour, cocoa, baking powder, salt, sugar, chocolate, eggs, and vanilla in a food processor; pulse to form a rough dough.
By hand, knead the hazelnuts into the dough. Divide the dough into 4 equal-sized pieces. Shape each piece into logs, 1in (2.5cm) thick and 12in (30cm) long. Place logs on floured baking sheets. Bake until firm to the touch, 25 minutes. Remove and allow to cool enough to handle. With a serrated knife, cut each log on the diagonal into ½in (1cm) thick slices. Place the slices in a single layer on baking sheets. Bake until crisp and dry, 15 minutes. Cool on a wire rack. Melt the white chocolate (see page 145). Fill piping bag with chocolate. Drizzle over the biscottini.

THINK AHEAD
Make up to 2 weeks in advance. Store in an airtight container at room temperature. Alternatively, freeze the unbaked biscotti logs up to 1 month in advance (see page 149). Defrost overnight in the refrigerator before baking.

COOKS' NOTE
For an alternative finish, try dipping one end of each biscottini into the melted white chocolate.

CURRY PUFFS

MAKES 35

1 recipe unbaked choux pastry
(see page 138)
1 tsp cumin seeds
2 tsp curry powder
1 tsp turmeric
¼ tsp cayenne pepper
½ onion, grated

Preheat oven to 350°F (180°C).
Toast cumin seeds in a dry pan over a
low heat until fragrant, 3 minutes.
Stir toasted spices and onion into pastry.
Drop teaspoonfuls on to a greased
baking sheet. Bake until golden, 30
minutes. Serve warm.

THINK AHEAD
Bake up to 3 days in advance. Store in an airtight
container at room temperature. Crisp in preheated
400˚F (200˚C) oven, 3 minutes.
Alternatively, bake and freeze up to 1 month in
advance (see page 149). Defrost. Crisp as directed.

CHORIZO PUFFS

MAKES 35

¼lb (125g) chorizo sausage, skinned and
finely chopped
1 recipe unbaked choux pastry
(see page 138)

Preheat oven to 350°F (180°C).
Stir chorizo into pastry. Drop
teaspoonfuls on to a greased baking
sheet. Bake until golden, 30 minutes.
Serve warm.

THINK AHEAD
Bake up to 3 days in advance. Store in an airtight
container at room temperature. Crisp in preheated
400˚F (200˚C) oven, 3 minutes.
Alternatively, bake and freeze up to 1 month in
advance (see page 149). Defrost. Crisp as directed.

MINI GOUGERES

MAKES 30

¾ cup (100g) grated gruyère cheese
1 recipe unbaked choux pastry
(see page 138)

ESSENTIAL EQUIPMENT
piping bag with large, plain tube

Preheat oven to 350°F (180°C).
Stir half of the cheese into the pastry.
Fill piping bag with pastry (see page
146) and pipe out rings, each one about
2in (5cm) in diameter, on to a greased
baking sheet. Sprinkle with remaining
cheese. Bake until golden, 30 minutes.
Serve warm.

THINK AHEAD
Bake up to 3 days in advance. Store in an airtight
container at room temperature. Crisp in preheated
400˚F (200˚C) oven, 3 minutes.
Alternatively, bake and freeze up to 1 month in
advance (see page 149). Defrost. Crisp as directed.

PARMESAN AND ANCHOVY PALMIERS

MAKES 20
½ of a 14oz package (250g) puff pastry
1¾ oz (50g) drained anchovy fillets, finely chopped
¼ tsp black pepper
2 tbsp grated parmesan cheese
1 egg yolk beaten with 1 tbsp water

Preheat oven to 400°C (200°F).
Roll pastry to 6in x 14in (15cm x 35cm) rectangle. Trim uneven edges with a sharp knife. Spread anchovies evenly over pastry. Sprinkle with pepper and parmesan. Roll up ends tightly to meet in the middle of pastry (see below). Refrigerate until firm, 20 minutes. Brush with beaten egg on all sides. Cut across into ½in (1cm) thick slices. Place slices on a greased baking sheet. Bake until crisp and golden, 10 minutes. Cool on wire rack. Serve warm or at room temperature.

THINK AHEAD
Same as recipes opposite.

Rolling up pastry for palmiers.

SUN-DRIED TOMATO PESTO PALMIERS

MAKES 20
6 sun-dried tomatoes packed in oil, drained (reserve oil) and finely chopped
1 garlic clove, crushed
1 tbsp reserved oil from sun-dried tomatoes
3 tbsp grated Parmesan cheese
½ of a 14oz package (250g) puff pastry
1 egg yolk beaten with 1 tbsp water

Preheat oven to 400°F (200°C).
For pesto, mix tomatoes, garlic, reserved oil, and 2 tbsp Parmesan until well combined. Roll pastry to 6in x 14in (15cm x 35cm) rectangle. Trim uneven edges with sharp knife. Spread pesto evenly over pastry. Roll up ends tightly to meet in the middle of pastry (see below, left). Refrigerate until firm, 20 minutes. Brush with beaten egg on all sides. Cut across into ½in (1cm) thick slices. Place slices on a greased baking sheet. Bake until crisp and golden, 10 minutes. Sprinkle with remaining Parmesan when hot from oven. Cool on wire rack. Serve warm or at room temperature.

THINK AHEAD
Bake up to 3 days in advance. Crisp in preheated 400°F (200°C), 3 minutes. Store in an airtight container at room temperature. Alternatively, freeze unbaked (see page 149). Bake from frozen in preheated 400°F (200°C) oven for 15 minutes.

HONEY MUSTARD AND PROSCIUTTO PALMIERS

MAKES 20
½ of a 14oz package (250g) puff pastry
2 tsp Dijon mustard
4 tsp honey
2½ oz (75g) sliced prosciutto
3 tbsp grated Parmesan cheese
1 egg yolk beaten with 1 tbsp water

Preheat oven to 400°F (200°C).
Roll pastry to 6in x 14in (15cm x 35cm) rectangle. Trim uneven edges with sharp knife. Combine mustard and honey. Spread evenly over pastry. Cover with sliced prosciutto. Sprinkle with 2 tbsp Parmesan. Roll up ends tightly to meet in the middle of pastry (see below, far left). Refrigerate until firm, 20 minutes. Brush with beaten egg on all sides. Cut across into ½in (1cm) slices. Place slices on a greased baking sheet. Bake until crisp and golden, 10 minutes. Sprinkle with remaining Parmesan when hot from oven. Cool on wire rack. Serve warm or at room temperature.

THINK AHEAD
Bake up to 3 days in advance. Crisp in preheated 400°F (200°C), 3 minutes. Store in an airtight container at room temperature. Alternatively, freeze unbaked (see page 149). Bake from frozen in preheated 400°F (200°C) for 15 minutes.

TWISTED PARSLEY BREADSTICKS

MAKES 35

1 recipe unbaked bread dough (see page 140)
3½oz (100g) red leicester or other hard orange cheese
1 cup (15g) flat-leaf parsley, roughly chopped
¼ tsp cayenne pepper

Preheat oven to 400°F (200°C).
Roll out dough to 6in x 20in (15cm x 50cm) rectangle. Sprinkle over cheese, parsley, and cayenne. Fold dough in half crosswise. Roll dough lightly to press in the filling and compress the two layers together. With a sharp knife, cut dough across into ¼in (0.5cm) wide strips. Hold ends of each strip between your fingers and twist ends in opposite directions. Lay twisted strips on to greased baking sheets (see below). Bake until crisp and golden, 15 minutes. Cool on wire rack. Serve warm or at room temperature.

THINK AHEAD
Bake up to 3 days in advance. Store in an airtight container at room temperature. Crisp in preheated 400°F (200°C) oven, 3 minutes.

PARMESAN CHEESE STRAWS

MAKES 40

½ of a 14oz package (250g) puff pastry
2 tsp paprika
3 tbsp grated Parmesan cheese
1 egg yolk beaten with 1 tbsp water

Preheat oven to 400°F (200°C).
Roll out pastry to 6in x 20in (15cm x 50cm) triangle. Sprinkle with paprika and 2 tbsp of the Parmesan. Spread cheese with your hands to evenly cover pastry. Fold pastry in half crosswise. Brush folded pastry with beaten egg. Sprinkle over remaining Parmesan. Press the cheese lightly into the pastry with hands.
With a sharp knife, cut pastry across into ¼in (0.5cm) wide strips. Hold the ends of each strip between your fingers and twist ends in opposite directions (see below, left). Lay twisted strips onto greased baking sheets. Bake until crisp and golden, 7 minutes. Cool on wire racks. Serve warm or at room temperature.

THINK AHEAD
Bake up to 3 days in advance. Store in airtight container at room temperature. Crisp in preheated 400°F (200°C) oven, 3 minutes.

VEGETABLE DIPPERS

Prepare your chosen vegetables as directed. Arrange vegetables in an air-tight container covered with damp paper towels. Cover with the lid and refrigerate. Serve chilled, with dips.

BABY CARROTS Choose firm, crisp baby carrots and use as quickly as possible because they spoil more quickly than regular carrots. Do not peel. Trim root end but leave a short green stem to act as a handle for dipping.

BABY POTATOES Choose even-sized, small new potatoes with a crisp, waxy texture and papery, thin skins. Simmer, unpeeled, in salted water until tender when pierced with the tip of a small sharp knife. Use both gold and red skinned potatoes for added color contrast.

CARROTS Avoid large carrots as they may have a tough, woody core. Organically grown carrots have the sweetest flavor. Cut into sticks about 3in (8cm) long and ¼in (0.5cm) thick.

CELERY Use only the pale, tender inner stalks. The outer stalks tend to be stringy and should be peeled. Cut into sticks about 3in (8cm) long and ¼in (0.5cm) thick.

CHICORY Trim the bitter stem end and use only the crisp, smaller inner leaves. Chicory is grown in red as well as white varieties.

CHERRY TOMATOES Try to find yellow as well as red for color contrast. The plum and pear shaped cherry tomato varieties are now widely available. Elongated shape are good for dipping.

CUCUMBERS Scrape out the seeds and discard. Cut into sticks about 3in (8cm) long and ¼in (0.5cm) thick. Leave unpeeled for color contrast between the dark green peel and pearly pale green interior.

RADISHES Trim the root end but leave a little green stem to act as a handle for dipping. Elongated French-style varieties with red tops and white tips are best for dipping.

THINK AHEAD
Prepare vegetables up to 1 day in advance.

COOKS' NOTE
Generous amounts of one or two vegetables make an impressive display. Use vegetables at their seasonal best rather than aiming for a broad selection.

FORMING TWISTED STRIPS
Twist ends in opposite directions

OVEN-DRIED ROOT AND FRUIT CHIPS

MAKES 2½ cups 150g

1 small sweet potato, unpeeled
1 small beet, unpeeled
1 small parsnip, unpeeled
1 apple, unpeeled
1 pear, unpeeled
2 tsp salt

ESSENTIAL EQUIPMENT
*either a food processor with a slicing
attachment, a mandoline, or a Japanese
vegetable slicer*

Preheat oven to 350°F (180°C).
Use either the slicing attachment or a
food processor, mandoline, or Japanese
vegetable slicer to slice the unpeeled
sweet potato, beet, parsnip, apple, and
pear ⅛in (2mm) thick. Place slices in a
single layer on greased baking sheets.
Put into the oven. Reduce oven
temperature to 250°F (120°C). Bake for
1½ hours, turning the slices over every
20 minutes, until dried. Cool in single
layers on wire racks. Sprinkle with salt.
Serve at room temperature, with or
without dips.

THINK AHEAD
Make up to 1 day in advance. Store in an airtight
container at room temperature.

CRISPY POTATO SKINS

MAKES 40
5 medium potatoes, punctured with fork
2 tbsp olive oil
1 tbsp finely chopped fresh rosemary
or 2 tsp crumbled dried rosemary
1½ tsp salt
1 tsp black pepper

Preheat oven to 350°F (180°C).
Bake potatoes until tender, 1 hour. Cool.
Cut each potato into 6 wedges. Scoop
out the cooked potato, leaving the skins
intact and a shell of potato and skin,
about ¼in (0.5cm) thick. If desired,
reserve cooked potato for another use.
Brush potato skins with oil on both
sides. Place in a single layer scooped
side up on to a wire rack set on top of a
9 x 13 baking pan. Sprinkle evenly with
rosemary, salt, and pepper. Bake for 15
minutes; then remove from oven and
turn skins over. Return skins to the oven
and continue baking until crisp and
golden brown, 15 minutes. Serve at
room temperature, with or without dips.

THINK AHEAD
Make up to 1 day in advance. Store in an airtight
container at room temperature.

COOK'S NOTE
Make this recipe the day before your party and use
the reserved cooked potato to make mashed potatoes for supper the night before.

HERBED PITA CRISPS

MAKES 40
2 garlic cloves, crushed
6 tbsp olive oil
4 pita breads, either white or whole wheat
2 tbsp fresh thyme leaves
or 2 tsp dried thyme
1½ tsp salt
1 tsp black pepper

ESSENTIAL EQUIPMENT
kitchen scissors or a serrated knife

Preheat oven to 350°F (180°C).
Stir garlic into oil. Cut each pita into
5 strips with scissors or a serrated knife.
Snip end of each strip and separate to
make 2 single layer strips. Place pita
strips split side up in a single layer on
baking sheets. Brush with garlic olive
oil. Sprinkle evenly with thyme, salt,
and pepper. Bake until crisp and golden
brown, 15 minutes. Cool. Serve at room
temperature with or without dips.

THINK AHEAD
Make up to 2 days in advance. Store in an airtight
container at room temperature.

COOKS' NOTE
To make spiced pita chips, sprinkle pita with
2 tsp each cumin and sesame seeds instead of thyme
leaves.

MINI CHICKEN DRUMSTICKS

20 chicken wings

ESSENTIAL EQUIPMENT
kitchen scissors or sharp boning knife

Cut the first joint of each chicken wing and discard wing tips. Holding small end of second joint, cut, scrape, and push meat down to thick end (see right). Pull skin and meat over end of bone with fingers to resemble baby drumsticks. Cut off knuckle end with scissors or knife. Repeat with remaining chicken wings.

THINK AHEAD
Make drumsticks up to 2 days in advance. Cover and refrigerate.

COOKS' NOTE
The tips and first joint of chicken wings are basically just skin and bone. When making drumsticks, reserve these parts for later use. They are ideal for making chicken stock.

HONEY MUSTARD CHICKEN WINGS

MAKES 20
8 garlic cloves, crushed
2 tbsp honey
2 tbsp Dijon mustard
2 tbsp light soy sauce
2 tbsp lemon juice
4 tbsp olive oil
2 tsp salt
1 tsp black pepper
1 recipe chicken wings (see above)

Combine garlic, honey, mustard, soy sauce, lemon, oil, salt, and pepper in a non-metallic bowl. Add chicken and toss to coat each piece well. Cover and refrigerate for at least 1 hour.
Preheat oven to 350°F (180°C).
Place chicken on a wire rack set over an oven tray. Bake until chicken is well browned and cooked through, 35 minutes.
Serve warm or at room temperature, with or without dips.

THINK AHEAD
Marinate chicken up to 1 day in advance. Cover and refrigerate.

GINGER HOISIN MINI CHICKEN DRUMSTICKS

MAKES 20
4in (10cm) piece fresh ginger, grated
2 garlic cloves, crushed
6 tbsp hoisin sauce
1 tbsp Chinese hot chili sauce
1 tbsp light soy sauce
1 tbsp sugar
1 tbsp water
1 recipe mini chicken drumsticks (see above)

Combine ginger, garlic, sauces, sugar, and water in a non-metallic bowl. Add chicken and toss to coat each piece well. Cover and refrigerate for at least 1 hour.
Preheat oven to 350°F (180°C).
Place chicken on a wire rack set over a baking pan. Bake until chicken is well browned and cooked through, 35 minutes.
Serve warm or at room temperature, with or without dips.

THINK AHEAD
Marinate chicken up to 1 day in advance. Cover and refrigerate.

HONEY SESAME GLAZED COCKTAIL SAUSAGES

MAKES ABOUT 30
1lb (500g) cocktail sausages, separated
1 tbsp sesame seeds
½ tbsp honey

Preheat oven to 350°F (180°C). Arrange the sausages in a single layer on a greased baking pan. Bake for 20 minutes, then turn sausages over on the pan. Roast until golden and cooked through, 15 minutes. Sprinkle with sesame seeds and drizzle with honey. Toss to coat each sausage well. Serve hot or warm, with or without dips.

THINK AHEAD
Cook sausages up to 12 hours in advance. Cool and cover with tin foil. Reheat in 400°F (200°C) oven, 10 minutes. Alternatively, cook sausages up to 1 hour in advance. Cover with foil and keep warm. Toss with seeds and honey just before serving.

COOKS' NOTE
If you can't find good quality cocktail sausages, use your favorite link sausages and cut into bite-sized pieces.

COCKTAIL SAUSAGE VARIATIONS

HONEY ROSEMARY GLAZED COCKTAIL SAUSAGES

Replace sesame seeds with 2 tsp finely chopped rosemary.

SWEET AND SPICY GLAZED COCKTAIL SAUSAGES

Replace honey and sesame seeds with 1½ tbsp mango chutney.

CURRY SPICED YOGURT, CILANTRO, AND MANGO CHUTNEY DIP

MAKES ABOUT 2 CUPS (500ml)
6 tbsp mango chutney
½ cup (1/2oz) cilantro, chopped
4 scallions, chopped
juice of 2 limes
¾ on an 8oz package (175g) cream cheese
1 cup (250g) yogurt
½ tsp curry powder
¼ tsp turmeric
salt, tabasco

Place chutney, cilantro, scallions, lime, cream cheese, yogurt, and spices in a food processor or blender; pulse until well blended. Add salt and tabasco to taste. Cover and refrigerate for 30 minutes to allow the flavors to blend. Serve chilled with dippers.

THINK AHEAD
Make dip up to 1 day in advance. Cover and refrigerate.

COOKS' NOTE
Make this creamy yogurt dip thai-style: omit the curry powder and replace the mango chutney with the same amount of thai sweet chili sauce.

SALSA ROMESCO DIP

MAKES ABOUT 2 CUPS (500ml)
1 red pepper, quartered and seeded
1 tbsp olive oil
½ cup (75g) blanched almonds
2in (5cm) thick slice of day-old bread, cubed
2 garlic cloves, chopped
¼ tsp cayenne pepper
½ tsp paprika
1 cup (15g) parsley, chopped
2 tomatoes, chopped
2 tbsp sherry vinegar
salt, black pepper

Broil and peel pepper quarters (see page 147). Heat oil in pan over a medium heat. Stir fry almonds and bread cubes until golden, 5 minutes. Drain on paper towels. Place peeled pepper quarters, almonds, bread, garlic, spices, parsley, tomatoes, and vinegar in a food processor or blender; pulse until well blended but still retaining some texture. If necessary, adjust the consistency by gradually adding water 1 tbsp at a time. Add salt and pepper to taste. Cover and refrigerate for 30 minutes to allow the flavors to blend. Serve chilled with dippers.

THINK AHEAD
Make dip up to 3 days in advance. Cover and refrigerate.

COOKS' NOTES
You don't have to restrict yourself to using almonds in this piquant Catalan sauce. You can use hazelnuts, pine nuts, or a combination of either with the almonds, with equal authenticity.

ROAST RED PEPPER, FETA AND MINT DIP

MAKES ABOUT 2 CUPS (500ml)
3 red peppers, quartered and seeded
1¾ cups (200g) feta cheese
1 8oz package (200g) cream cheese
1 garlic clove, chopped
3 tbsp finely chopped fresh mint
2 tbsp olive oil
1 tbsp lemon juice
salt, black pepper

Broil and peel pepper quarters (see page 147). Place peeled pepper quarters, feta and cream cheese, garlic, mint, oil, and lemon juice in a food processor or blender; pulse until well blended but still retaining some texture. If necessary, adjust consistency by gradually adding water 1 tbsp at a time. Add salt and pepper to taste. Cover and refrigerate for 30 minutes to allow the flavors to blend. Serve chilled with dippers.

THINK AHEAD
Make dip up to 3 days in advance. Cover and refrigerate.

AVOCADO LIME CREAM DIP

MAKES ABOUT 2 CUPS (500ml)
2 medium avocados
4 scallions, chopped
2 green chilies, seeded and finely chopped
½ cup (15g) cilantro
juice of 2 limes
1 tbsp olive oil
⅔ cup (150ml) sour cream
salt

Place avocado, scallions, chilies, cilantro, lime, olive oil, and sour cream in a food processor or blender; pulse until smooth. Add salt to taste. Cover and refrigerate for 15 minutes to allow the flavors to blend. Serve chilled with dippers.

THINK AHEAD
Make dip up to 8 hours ahead. Cover and refrigerate.

COOKS' NOTE
To prevent the avocado cream dip from discoloring, make sure you press a piece of plastic wrap directly on to the surface of the dip. It's the oxygen in the air that turns avocado brown, so the less air that comes into contact with the dip, the better.

HERBED YOGURT DIP

MAKES ABOUT 2 CUPS (500ml)

1 cup (15g) parsley, chopped
1 cup (15g) basil, chopped
½ cup (15g) chives, chopped
grated peel of ½ lemon
juice of 1 lemon
¾ of an 8oz package (175g) cream cheese
1 cup (250g) whole milk yogurt
3 tbsp olive oil
salt, black pepper

Place herbs, lemon juice and peel, cream cheese, yogurt, and oil in a food processor or blender; pulse until well blended. Add salt and pepper to taste. Cover and refrigerate for 30 minutes to allow the flavors to blend. Serve chilled.

THINK AHEAD
Make dip up to 1 day in advance. Cover and refrigerate.

COOKS' NOTE
Use your favorite bouquet of green herbs to flavor this fragrant dip. Choose from arrugula, tarragon, marjoram, chervil, watercress, or lovage instead of one or all of our favorite combination of parsley, basil, and chives.
For a lighter dip, use ricotta cheese in place of some or all of the cream cheese.

CREAMY BLUE CHEESE AND SCALLION DIP

MAKES ABOUT 2 CUPS (500ml)

6 scallions, chopped
1¾ cups (200g) blue cheese
(see cooks' note)
1¼ cups (300ml) sour cream
1 tsp Worcestershire sauce
salt, black pepper

Place scallions, cheese, sour cream, and Worcestershire sauce in a food processor or blender; pulse until well blended but still retaining some texture. If necessary, adjust consistency by gradually adding water 1 tbsp at a time. Add salt and pepper to taste. Cover and refrigerate for 30 minutes to allow the flavors to blend. Serve chilled.

THINK AHEAD
Make dip up to 1 day in advance. Cover and refrigerate. Let stand at room temperature for 15 minutes to soften slightly before serving.

COOKS' NOTE
Your choice of blue cheese will determine the richness and piquancy of this delicious dip. Use roquefort, gorgonzola, or stilton to intensify its zesty, pungent flavor. Try dolcelatte or danish blue to make a dip with a milder, mellower taste.

SUN-DRIED TOMATO AND CANNELLINI BEAN DIP

MAKES ABOUT 2 CUPS (500ml)

15½oz (400g) can of cannellini beans, drained
8 sun-dried tomatoes in oil, drained (about 14 oz)
1 garlic clove, chopped
1 tbsp chopped rosemary
4 tbsp olive oil
2 tbsp red wine vinegar
½ cup (125ml) water
salt, black pepper

Place beans, sun-dried tomatoes, garlic, rosemary, oil, vinegar, and water in a food processor or blender; pulse to a smooth purée. If necessary, adjust the consistency by gradually adding more water, 1 tbsp at a time. Add salt and pepper to taste. Cover and refrigerate for 30 minutes to allow the flavors to blend. Serve chilled.

THINK AHEAD
Make dip up to 3 days in advance. Cover and refrigerate.

COOKS' NOTE
Cannellini are slender, ivory white Italian beans. Their creamy texture and their ability to absorb strong, aromatic flavors makes them ideal for dips. If you cannot find a source for cannellini beans, any canned white bean will make an excellent substitute.

SPICY PEANUT DIP

MAKES ABOUT 2 CUPS (500ml)

1 cup (250g) peanut butter
2 garlic cloves, crushed
1in (2.5cm) piece fresh ginger, grated
juice of 1 lemon
4 tbsp soy sauce
2 tbsp honey
1 tsp turmeric
1 tsp tabasco
½ cup (125ml) water
salt, black pepper

Place peanut butter, garlic, ginger, lemon, soy sauce, honey, turmeric, tabasco, and water in a food processor or blender; pulse until smooth. If necessary, adjust consistency by gradually adding extra water 1 tbsp at a time. Add salt and pepper to taste. Cover and refrigerate for 30 minutes to allow the flavors to blend. Serve chilled.

THINK AHEAD
Make dip up to 3 days in advance. Cover and refrigerate.

SPICED ROASTED EGGPLANT DIP

MAKES ABOUT 2 CUPS (500ml)

2 medium eggplants, pierced with fork
1 garlic clove, crushed
4 tbsp tahini
½ tsp ground cumin
1 tbsp lemon juice
½ cup (125ml) whole-milk yogurt
salt, cayenne pepper

Preheat oven to 400°F (200°C).
Place eggplant on a baking pan and roast until skin is blistered and flesh is soft, 45 minutes. When cool, peel off charred skin and squeeze out as much moisture as possible. Place eggplant and garlic in a food processor or blender; pulse until smooth. Add tahini, cumin, lemon, and yogurt; pulse to a smooth purée. Add salt and cayenne pepper to taste. Cover and refrigerate for 30 minutes to allow the flavors to blend. Serve chilled with dippers.

THINK AHEAD
Make dip up to 3 days in advance. Cover and refrigerate.

COOKS' NOTE
For an extra smoky flavor, broil the eggplants directly over an open flame (either a grill or gas burner) until blackened on all sides. Peel and squeeze as directed.

TOPS AND BOTTOMS

TINY PARMESAN SHORTBREADS

MAKES 40

⅓ cup (60g) all-purpose flour, sifted
salt, cayenne pepper
3 tbsp (45g) cold butter, diced
⅔ cup (60g) parmesan cheese, grated

ESSENTIAL EQUIPMENT

1½ in (3.5cm) fluted pastry cutter, baking parchment

Preheat oven to 350°F (180°C). Place flour, a pinch each salt and cayenne, butter, parmesan, and any additional flavoring, if using, in a food processor; pulse to form a smooth dough. Roll out dough on a floured surface to a ¼ in (0.5cm) thickness. Cut out 40 rounds with the pastry cutter. Place dough rounds on parchment lined baking sheets ¾ in (2cm) apart and refrigerate for 30 minutes. Bake until golden brown, 8 minutes. Cool completely on a wire rack before topping.

THINK AHEAD
Bake shortbreads up to 2 weeks in advance. Store in an airtight container. Alternatively, bake and freeze up to 1 month in advance. Defrost and crisp in preheated 400°F (200°C) oven for 3 minutes.

FLAVORED VARIATIONS

PARMESAN AND ROSEMARY SHORTBREADS

Add 1 tsp dried rosemary to the ingredients.

PARMESAN AND BLACK OLIVE SHORTBREADS

Add 1 tsp finely chopped black olives to the ingredients.

TINY PARMESAN AND ROSEMARY SHORTBREADS WITH ROASTED CHERRY TOMATOES AND FETA

MAKES 40

20 cherry tomatoes, halved
2 tsp olive oil
½ tsp honey
salt, black pepper
1 cup (125g) feta cheese, crumbled
5 pitted black olives, quartered
1 recipe tiny parmesan and rosemary shortbreads (see opposite)

Preheat oven to 400°F (200°C). Place tomato halves on a baking pan and sprinkle with oil, honey, salt, and pepper. Roast in oven until softened, 20 minutes.
Top shortbreads with tomatoes and feta. Garnish with olives. Serve at room temperature.

THINK AHEAD
Prepare tomatoes up to 1 day in advance. Cover and refrigerate. Bring to room temperature before using. Top shortbreads up to 2 hours before serving.

TINY PARMESAN AND BLACK OLIVE SHORTBREADS WITH PARSLEY PESTO AND GOAT CHEESE

MAKES 40

½ cup (15g) parsley
2 tbsp pine nuts
4 tbsp parmesan cheese, grated
1 garlic clove, crushed
1 tbsp olive oil
salt, black pepper
⅓ cup (100g) fresh creamy goat cheese
20 parsley leaves
1 recipe tiny parmesan and black olive shortbreads (see opposite)

Place parsley, pine nuts, parmesan, garlic, and oil in a food processor or blender; pulse to a thick paste. Add salt and pepper to taste. Use a teaspoon to top shortbreads with pesto and goat's cheese. Serve at room temperature.

THINK AHEAD
Make pesto up to 3 days in advance. Top shortbreads up to 2 hours before serving.

COCKTAIL CORN CAKES WITH SPICY MANGO SALSA

MAKES 20

FOR PANCAKES

3 tbsp medium cornmeal
½ cup (60g) all-purpose flour
¼ tsp salt
¼ tsp baking powder
1 egg, beaten
5 tbsp milk
1 tbsp melted butter
⅔ cup (125g) corn kernels
cayenne pepper
1 tbsp sunflower oil

FOR SALSA

½ mango, finely diced
(see page 163)
½ medium red onion, finely
chopped
1 fresh green chili, seeded and
finely diced
juice of 1 lime
salt, black pepper
½ cup (125ml) crème fraîche
20 cilantro leaves to garnish

Mix the cornmeal, flour, salt baking powder, egg, milk, and butter to make a smooth batter. Stir in corn kernels. Add cayenne pepper to taste.

Brush a frying pan or griddle with oil. Preheat over medium heat. Working in batches, drop heaped teaspoonfuls of mixture onto the hot surface. Cook until crisp and golden, 2½ minutes per side. Brush pan with oil between each batch of pancakes. Cool pancakes to room temperature.

For salsa, combine mango, onion, chili, and lime. Add salt and pepper to taste. Top each cake with 1 teaspoonful each crème fraîche and salsa. Garnish with cilantro leaves. Serve at room temperature.

THINK AHEAD
Make cakes up to 1 day in advance. Store in an airtight container in the refrigerator. Crisp in preheated 400°F (200°C) oven for 3 minutes. Make salsa up to 5 hours in advance. Cover and refrigerate. Top pancakes 45 minutes before serving.

COOKS' NOTE
The best flavor comes from fresh corn. Scrape kernels off the cob with a sharp knife. Use canned corn, drained, or frozen corn, defrosted, when fresh is not available.

WILD RICE AND SCALLION PANCAKES WITH AVOCADO LIME SALSA

MAKES 20

FOR PANCAKES

4 tbsp wild rice
2 tbsp basmati rice
½ cup (60g) all-purpose flour
¼ tsp salt
1 egg, beaten
4 tbsp milk
2 tbsp finely chopped scallion
1 tbsp sunflower oil

FOR SALSA

1 small avocado, finely diced
½ medium red onion, finely
chopped
juice of 1 lime
1 tbsp olive oil
salt, tabasco
2 scallions, white stems only, to
garnish

Cook each type of rice in a separate pan of boiling water until tender; wild rice, for 40 minutes, basmati rice, for 12 minutes. Drain and cool. Mix the flour, salt, egg, and milk together to make a smooth batter. Stir both types of cooked rice and the chopped scallions into the batter.

Brush a frying pan or griddle with oil. Preheat over medium heat. Working in batches, drop heaped teaspoonfuls of mixture onto the hot surface. Cook until crisp and golden, 2½ minutes per side. Brush pan with oil between each batch of pancakes. Cool pancakes to room temperature.

For salsa, combine avocado, onion, lime, and oil. Add salt and tabasco to taste. For garnish, cut scallions into 1½ in (3.5cm) pieces. Cut each piece into quarters lengthwise.

Top pancakes with equal amounts of salsa. Garnish each pancake with a slice of a scallion. Serve at room temperature.

THINK AHEAD
Make pancakes up to 1 day in advance. Store in an airtight container in the refrigerator. Crisp in preheated 400°F (200°C) oven, 3 minutes. Make salsa up to 2 hours in advance. Cover and refrigerate. Top pancakes 45 minutes before serving.

HERB PANCAKES

MAKES 20

½ cup (60g) all-purpose flour
¼ tsp baking powder
¼ tsp salt
1 egg, beaten
3 tbsp milk
1 tbsp finely chopped fresh herbs
1 tbsp sunflower oil

Sift flour, baking powder, and salt together. Make a well in the center. Add egg and milk to well. Gradually stir in the flour and mix to a smooth batter. Stir in herbs (see below). Brush a frying pan or griddle with oil. Preheat over medium heat. Working in batches, drop heaped teaspoonfuls of mixture onto the hot surface. Cook until bubbles appear and underside is golden, 3 minutes. Turn and brown other side, 2 minutes. Brush pan with oil between each batch of pancakes. Cool pancakes. Serve at room temperature.

THINK AHEAD
Make pancakes up to 2 days in advance. Store in an airtight container in the refrigerator. Crisp in preheated 400°F (200°C) oven for 3 minutes.

VARIATIONS
DILL PANCAKES

Add 1 tbsp finely chopped dill to the ingredients.

CHIVE PANCAKES

Add 1 tbsp finely chopped chives to the ingredients.

DILL PANCAKES WITH SALMON CAVIAR AND LEMON CREME FRAICHE

MAKES 20

1 tsp grated lemon peel
1 tbsp lemon juice
½ cup (125ml) crème fraîche
1 recipe dill pancakes (see above)
3½oz (100g) salmon caviar
20 dill sprigs to garnish

Mix lemon peel and juice into crème fraîche. Top each pancake with 1 teaspoonful each crème fraîche and salmon caviar. Garnish with dill. Serve at room temperature.

THINK AHEAD
Make lemon crème fraîche up to 1 day in advance. Cover and refrigerate. Top pancakes up to 45 minutes before serving.

CHIVE PANCAKES WITH CREME FRAICHE AND RED ONION CONFIT

MAKES 20

2 tbsp sugar
1 tbsp water
1 tbsp red wine vinegar
1 medium red onion, finely sliced
salt, black pepper
1 recipe chive pancakes (see opposite)
½ cup (125ml) crème fraîche
1 tbsp finely chopped fresh chives to garnish

Put sugar and water in a small pan and stir to dissolve. Bring to a boil over medium-low heat and cook to a dark caramel (see page 145). Remove from heat and add vinegar and onions. Return to medium heat and stir fry until onions soften, 5 minutes. Add salt and pepper to taste. Cool to warm. Top each pancake with 1 teaspoonful each crème fraîche and onions. Garnish with chives. Serve at room temperature.

THINK AHEAD
Make onion confit up to 1 day in advance. Cover and store at room temperature. Top pancakes up to 45 minutes before serving.

BUCKWHEAT BLINIS WITH SOUR CREAM AND CAVIAR

MAKES 20

1 cup (100g) buckwheat flour
¼ tsp baking powder
¼ tsp salt
1 egg, separated
½ cup (100ml) milk
½ cup (125ml) sour cream
3½oz (100g) caviar

Sift flour, baking powder, and salt together. Make a well in the center of the flour. Beat egg yolk and milk. Add to the well. Gradually stir the flour into the egg mixture. Mix to a smooth batter. Beat egg white until it holds soft peaks (see page 141). Gently fold the beaten egg white into the batter. Brush a frying pan or griddle with oil. Preheat over medium heat. Working in batches, drop heaped teaspoonfuls of mixture onto the hot surface. Cook until bubbles appear and underside is golden, 3 minutes. Turn and brown other side, 2 minutes. Brush pan with oil between each batch of blinis. Cool blinis before topping. Top each blini with 1 teaspoonful each sour cream and caviar. Serve at room temperature.

THINK AHEAD
Make blinis up to 2 days in advance. Store in airtight container in refrigerator. Crisp in preheated 400°F (200°C) oven, 3 minutes. Top up to 30 minutes before serving.

CROSTINI

MAKES 20
20 slices day-old baguette, ½ in (1cm)
thick
4 tbsp olive oil

Preheat oven to 350°F (180°C).
Place baguette slices on a baking
sheet. Brush with olive oil. Bake until
crisp and lightly golden, 10 minutes.
Serve plain or topped according to
the following recipes.

THINK AHEAD
Make crostini up to 2 weeks in advance. Cool
completely and store in an airtight container
at room temperature.

COOKS' NOTE
Choose a thin baguette about 2-3in (5-8cm) in
diameter. Add a crushed clove of garlic to the oil
before brushing the bread for extra flavor.

SPICY SHRIMP CROSTINI

MAKES 20
about ½lb (200g) medium shrimp
½ medium red onion, finely chopped
1 garlic clove, crushed
½ tsp crushed chili flakes
2 tbsp olive oil
1 tbsp lemon juice
salt, black pepper
1 tbsp finely chopped parsley
1 recipe crostini (see opposite)

Combine shrimp with onion, garlic,
chili, oil, and lemon. Add salt and
pepper to taste and stir in parsley.
Spoon on to crostini. Serve at
room temperature.

THINK AHEAD
Make topping up to 1 day in advance, but add salt,
pepper, and parsley just before serving for the best
texture and color. Store in an airtight container in the
refrigerator. Top crostini up to 1 hour before
serving.

TOMATO AND BASIL CROSTINI

MAKES 20
5 ripe plum tomatoes, seeded and diced
(see page 147)
½ medium red onion, finely chopped
1 garlic clove, crushed
2 tbsp olive oil
1 tbsp balsamic vinegar
salt, black pepper
1 recipe crostini (see opposite)
20 basil leaves to garnish

Mix tomato, onion, garlic, oil, and
vinegar together. Add salt and pepper to
taste. Spoon onto crostini. Garnish with
basil leaves. Serve at room temperature.

THINK AHEAD
Make topping up to 1 day in advance, but add the
salt and pepper just before serving. Store in an airtight container in the refrigerator. Top crostini up to
45 minutes before serving.

COOKS' NOTE
Basil is the tomato's classic culinary partner. Try
arugula in place of basil for a deep, peppery bite. Stir
in a handful of sliced arugula just before serving.
Reserve some smaller leaves for the garnish.

WHITE BEAN AND SAGE CROSTINI

MAKES 20
3 tbsp olive oil
1 small onion, finely chopped
2 garlic cloves, finely chopped
4 sage leaves, finely chopped
15½oz (400g) can cannellini beans, drained
2 tbsp water
salt, black pepper
1 recipe crostini (see page 42)
1 seeded ripe tomato, diced (see page 147)
extra olive oil for drizzling

Heat oil in a saucepan. Add onion, garlic, and sage and cook over low heat until soft, about 5 minutes. Add beans, water, and salt and pepper to taste. Cook for about 10 minutes. Mash the beans with a wooden spoon to make a rough purée. Spread bean purée on crostini. Top each crostini with a little tomato dice and a drizzle of olive oil. Serve warm or at room temperature.

THINK AHEAD
Make topping up to 3 days in advance. Cover and refrigerate. Return to room temperature before serving. Top crostini up to 1 hour before serving.

AVOCADO AND GOAT CHEESE CROSTINI

MAKES 20
1 large avocado
⅔ cup (150g) fresh creamy goat cheese
grated peel and juice of 1 lemon
1 tbsp olive oil
salt, tabasco
1 recipe crostini (see page 42)

Place avocado, cheese, peel, juice, and oil in a food processor or blender; pulse to a smooth purée. Add salt and tabasco to taste. Spoon topping on to each crostini. Serve at room temperature.

THINK AHEAD
Make topping up to 6 hours in advance. Store in a bowl covered with plastic wrap, pressing directly onto purée to prevent contact with air and discoloration. Keep refrigerated and stir before using. Top crostini up to 20 minutes before serving.

EGGPLANT CAVIAR CROSTINI

MAKES 20
2 medium eggplants, pierced with a fork
1 garlic clove, crushed
juice of ½ lemon
2 tbsp olive oil
1 tbsp whole-milk yogurt
salt, cayenne pepper
1 recipe crostini (see page 42)
20 mint sprigs to garnish
1 tsp paprika to garnish

Broil eggplant until the skin is black and blistered and the flesh feels soft. When cool enough to handle, peel off charred skin. Use hands to squeeze out as much moisture as possible from the flesh. Place eggplant, garlic, lemon, oil, and yogurt in a food processor or blender; pulse to a smooth purée. Add salt and cayenne pepper to taste. Cool completely. Spoon topping on to each crostini. Garnish with mint sprigs and a pinch of paprika. Serve at room temperature.

THINK AHEAD
Make topping up to 2 days in advance. Cover and refrigerate. Top crostini up to 45 minutes before serving.

MINI CHERRY TOMATO AND BASIL PESTO GALETTES

MAKES 20

½ cup (15g) basil
2 tbsp pine nuts
1 tbsp olive oil
4 tbsp parmesan cheese, grated
½ of a 14oz package (200g) puff pastry
20 cherry tomatoes, each cut into 3 slices
salt, black pepper
20 basil sprigs to garnish

ESSENTIAL EQUIPMENT
2in (5cm) fluted pastry cutter

For pesto, place basil, pine nuts, oil, and parmesan in a food processor or blender; pulse to a thick paste. Preheat oven to 400°F (200°C). Roll out pastry on a floured surface to a ⅛in (0.25cm) thickness. Cut out 20 rounds with the pastry cutter. Place pastry rounds on to a floured baking sheet. Spread ½ tsp pesto on to each pastry round and top with 3 cherry tomato slices. Sprinkle with salt and pepper. Bake until crisp and golden, 10 minutes. Garnish each galette with ½ tsp pesto and a basil sprig. Serve warm.

THINK AHEAD
Make pesto up to 3 days in advance. Cover and refrigerate. Bake galettes up to 1 day in advance. Reheat in preheated 400°F (200°C) oven for 3 minutes. Garnish and serve warm.

MINI MANGO GALETTES

MAKES 20

½ of a 14oz package (200g) puff pastry
200g (7oz) tin of sliced mangoes, drained
2 tbsp apricot jam
2 tsp powdered sugar for dusting

Preheat oven to 400°F (200°C).
Roll out pastry on a floured surface to a ⅛in (0.25cm) thickness. Cut pastry into approximately 20 squares, measuring 2in x 2in (5cm x 5cm) each. Trace a fine line inside each square using a sharp knife (see below, left). Be careful not to actually cut through the pastry. Pierce the center of each square with a fork (see below, right). Place pastry squares on a floured baking sheet. Cut mango slices into ¼in (0.5cm) thick pieces. Arrange 2 or 3 mango pieces, slightly overlapping, on top of each pastry square. Dust with powdered sugar. Bake until pastry is crisp and golden, 10 minutes. Stir apricot jam with 1 tbsp water over low heat, melting to form a glaze. Allow galettes to cool; then brush with the apricot glaze. Serve at room temperature.

THINK AHEAD
Same as mini apple galettes.

MINI APPLE GALETTES

MAKES 20

½ of a 14oz package (200g) puff pastry
2 apples, quartered and cored
2 tsp powdered sugar
2 tbsp apricot jam

ESSENTIAL EQUIPMENT
2in (5cm) plain pastry cutter

Preheat oven to 400°F (200°C).
Roll out pastry on a floured surface to a ⅛in (0.25cm) thickness. Cut out 20 rounds with the pastry cutter. Place them on a floured baking sheet.
Cut each apple quarter across into fine slices. Arrange apple slices, slightly overlapping, on each pastry round. Dust with powdered sugar. Bake until pastry is crisp and golden, 10 minutes. Melt apricot jam with 1 tbsp water over low heat to make glaze. Allow galettes to cool, then brush with apricot glaze. Serve at room temperature.

THINK AHEAD
Make up to 1 day in advance. Glaze up to 5 hours in advance.

Trace a fine line using a sharp knife.

Prick center with a fork.

ROAST RED ONION AND THYME FOCACCINE

MAKES 20

**1 recipe unbaked bread dough
(see page 140)
1 cup (125g) gruyère cheese, grated
1 medium red onion, quartered
coarse salt, black pepper
3 thyme sprigs, roughly chopped**

ESSENTIAL EQUIPMENT
2in (5cm) plain pastry cutter

Preheat oven to 400°F (200°C).
Roll out dough on a floured surface to a
¼in (0.5cm) thickness. Cut out 20
rounds with the pastry cutter. Place on
to a floured baking sheet and sprinkle
with cheese. Cut each onion quarter
across into 5 slices. Place a slice on top
of each round. Sprinkle with salt,
pepper, and thyme. Bake until crisp and
golden, 15 minutes. Serve warm.

THINK AHEAD
Bake up to 1 day in advance. Store in an airtight
container at room temperature. Crisp in preheated
400°F (200°C) oven for 10 minutes. Alternatively,
assemble and freeze unbaked for up to 1 month (see
page 149). Bake from frozen in preheated 400°F
(200°C) oven for 20 minutes.

POTATO AND ROSEMARY FOCACCINE

MAKES 20

**20 very small new potatoes
1 recipe unbaked bread dough
(see page 140)
1 cup (125g) gruyère cheese, grated
½ tsp salt, ¼ tsp black pepper
3 rosemary sprigs, separated into 20 pieces
(see page 147)**

ESSENTIAL EQUIPMENT
2in (5cm) plain pastry cutter

Preheat oven to 400°F (200°C).
Cut potatoes into ¼in (0.5cm) thick
slices. Place potato slices in boiling
water and cook for 5 minutes from the
time the water has returned to a boil.
Drain and cool. Roll out dough on a
floured surface to a ¼in (0.5cm)
thickness. Cut out 20 rounds with the
pastry cutter. Place on to a floured
baking sheet. Sprinkle all the rounds
evenly with about three quarters of the
cheese. Arrange 4 potato slices on top of
each round. Sprinkle over the remaining
cheese and salt and pepper. Top each
round with a tuft of rosemary. Bake until
crisp and golden, 15 minutes. Serve warm.

THINK AHEAD
Bake up to 1 day in advance. Store in an airtight
container at room temperature. Crisp in preheated
400°F (200°C) oven for 10 minutes. Alternatively,
assemble and freeze unbaked for up to 1 month (see
page 149). Bake from frozen in preheated 400°F
(200°C) oven for 20 minutes.

ARTICHOKE AND GORGONZOLA FOCACCINE

MAKES 20

**1 recipe unbaked bread dough
(see page 140)
1 cup (125g) gorgonzola or danish blue
cheese, crumbled
salt, black pepper
20 baby artichokes hearts in oil, drained
and halved
2 tbsp finely chopped oregano**

ESSENTIAL EQUIPMENT
2in (5cm) plain pastry cutter

Preheat oven to 400°F (200°C).
Roll out dough on a floured surface to a
¼in (0.5cm) thickness. Cut out 20
rounds with the pastry cutter. Place on
to a floured baking sheet. Sprinkle each
round with cheese, salt and pepper. Top
with 2 artichoke halves. Bake until crisp
and golden, 15 minutes. Garnish with
chopped oregano and serve warm.

THINK AHEAD
Bake up to 1 day in advance. Store in an airtight
container at room temperature. Crisp in preheated
400°F (200°C) oven for 10 minutes. Alternatively,
assemble and freeze unbaked for up to 1 month (see
page 149). Bake from frozen in preheated 400°F
(200°C) oven for 20 minutes.

CROUTES

MAKES 20
7 medium slices white bread

ESSENTIAL EQUIPMENT
2in (5cm) fluted pastry cutter

Preheat oven to 300°F
(150°C).

Cut out each slice into 3
rounds. Place on a baking
sheet and bake until crisp,
25 minutes. Cool.

THINK AHEAD
Make up to 3 days in advance.
Store in an airtight container at
room temperature.

BROILED BEEF FILLET WITH SALSA VERDE CROUTES

MAKES 20
¾ cup (15g) parsley
10 basil leaves
10 mint leaves
1 garlic clove, crushed
1 tbsp dijon mustard
1 tbsp drained capers
2 drained anchovy fillets
2 tbsp olive oil
salt and black pepper
¾lb (350g) beef fillet steak, ¾in (1.5cm) thick
1 recipe croutes (see above)

ESSENTIAL EQUIPMENT
½in (2.5cm) plain pastry cutter, cast-iron grill pan

For salsa, place fresh herbs, garlic, mustard, capers, anchovies, and oil in a food processor or blender; pulse to a thick paste. Add salt and pepper to taste. Cut steak into 20 rounds with a pastry cutter (see below). Preheat grill pan over high heat. Sear steak rounds, about 3 minutes per side. Sprinkle with salt and pepper. Place one round on to each croute. Top with salsa. Serve warm or at room temperature.

FRESH SALMON TARTARE CROUTES

MAKES 20
½lb (250g) fresh salmon fillet
juice of 1 lemon
2 tbsp drained cornichons, finely chopped
2 tbsp drained capers, finely chopped
1 tbsp mayonnaise (see page 142)
1 tsp grainy mustard
1 tbsp finely chopped tarragon
½ tsp salt
½ tsp tabasco
½ lemon, peeled (see page 147)
1 recipe croutes (see above)

Cut salmon into fine dice and place in a bowl. Toss salmon pieces with lemon juice to coat. Cover and refrigerate for 3 hours. Drain off lemon juice and discard. Add cornichons, capers, mayonnaise, mustard, tarragon, and salt to salmon. Stir to coat. Add tabasco to taste. Cut lemon into wedges (see below). Spoon salmon tartare on to croutes. Garnish with lemon wedges. Served chilled.

THINK AHEAD
Prepare topping up to 1 day in advance. Cover and refrigerate. Top croutes up to 30 minutes in advance. Garnish and serve chilled.

CUTTING OUT STEAK ROUNDS

LEMON SEGMENTS
Cut lemon half into 4 slices.

Cut each slice into wedges.

BROILED SCALLOPS WITH SWEET CHILI SAUCE AND CREME FRAICHE

MAKES 20

10 sea scallops
salt, black pepper
4 tbsp thai sweet chili sauce
1 recipe croutes (see page 46)
6 tbsp crème fraîche
20 cilantro leaves to garnish

ESSENTIAL EQUIPMENT
cast-iron grill pan

Cut each scallop in half. Preheat grill pan over high heat. Sear scallops, 1 minute per side. Sprinkle with salt and pepper to taste and toss with chili sauce. Place 1 scallop half on to each croute. Top with 1 tsp crème fraîche. Garnish with cilantro leaves. Serve at room temperature or chilled.

THINK AHEAD
Sear and sauce scallops up to 1 day in advance. Cover and refrigerate. Top croutes up to 1 hour in advance.

COOKS' NOTE
For an even better flavor, barbecue the scallops 3in (8cm) above medium hot coals. Cook for 1 minute per side.

SEARED TUNA NICOISE CROUTES

MAKES 20

½lb (200g) tuna steak, 1in (2.5cm) thick
salt, black pepper
½ romaine heart, leaves separated
10 green beans
1 tomato, seeded and diced (see page 147)
2 tbsp drained baby capers
10 anchovy fillets, roughly chopped
10 pitted black olives, sliced
2 tbsp olive oil
1 tbsp red wine vinegar
salt, black pepper
1 recipe croutes (see page 46)
2 tbsp mayonnaise (see page 142)

ESSENTIAL EQUIPMENT
cast-iron grill pan.

Cut tuna into 1in (2.5cm) cubes. Preheat grill pan over high heat. Sear tuna cubes on both sides until firm to the touch, 2 minutes per side. Season with salt and pepper. Cool. Cut stalks from salad leaves and discard. Cut each leaf into 1in (2.5cm) pieces. Cut beans into ½in (1cm) lengths. Put beans into a pan of boiling water. After the water returns to a boil, drain the beans and refresh in cold water. Pat dry with paper towels. Toss beans, tomato, capers, anchovies, and olives with oil and vinegar. Add salt and pepper to taste. Spread each croute with mayonnaise and top with a salad leaf. Place a cube of tuna on top. Garnish with vegetables. Serve at room temperature.

THINK AHEAD
Prepare vegetables up to 1 day in advance. Cover and refrigerate. Cook tuna up to 2 hours in advance. Keep at room temperature until ready to assemble. Top croutes up to 1 hour in advance.

ASPARAGUS CROUTES WITH LEMON HOLLANDAISE

MAKES 20

10 medium asparagus tips, halved lengthwise
¾ cup (15g) chives
1 recipe lemon hollandaise (see page 143)
1 recipe croutes (see page 46)
1 tsp paprika to dust

Put asparagus in to a pan of boiling water. Once the water returns to a boil, drain asparagus and refresh immediately in cold water. Pat dry with kitchen paper. Cut chives on the diagonal into 1in (2.5cm) lengths. Spoon hollandaise on to croutes and top with asparagus halves. Dust with paprika. Garnish with chives. Serve at room temperature.

THINK AHEAD
Cook asparagus up to 1 day in advance. Cover and refrigerate. Top croutes up to 1 hour in advance.

TINY SCONES

MAKES 10
1⅛ cups (175g) all-purpose flour
1½ tsp baking powder
pinch of salt
3 tbsp (45g) butter, diced
1½ tbsp sugar
1 egg, beaten
¼ cup (60ml) cream

ESSENTIAL EQUIPMENT
1½ in (4cm) fluted pastry cutter

Preheat oven to 400°F (200°C).

Sift flour, baking powder, and salt. Crumble the butter into the flour with fingertips until mixture resembles fine crumbs. Stir in sugar (omit if making savory scones) and any additional flavoring, if using. With a fork, mix in the egg and enough cream to make a soft dough. Turn dough onto a floured surface and knead lightly until smooth. Gently roll out to a 1in (2.5cm) thickness and cut out 10 rounds with the pastry cutter. Place rounds on a greased and floured baking sheet. Bake until firm and golden, 8-10 minutes . Cool on a wire rack.

VARIATIONS
TINY DILL SCONES
Replace sugar with 1 tbsp finely chopped dill.

TINY HEART-SHAPED SCONES
Cut out dough with a 2½ in (6cm) heart-shaped pastry cutter.

THINK AHEAD
Bake scones up to 1 week in advance. Store in an airtight container at room temperature.

COOKS' NOTE
Cover the scones with a cloth while they cool on the wire rack. This will keep some of the steam in, making the scones soft, moist, and light.

TINY DILL SCONES WITH SMOKED TROUT AND HORSERADISH CREAM

MAKES 20
1 recipe tiny dill scones (see above)
½ cup (125ml) sour cream
1 tbsp horseradish sauce
5oz (150g) smoked trout slices
black pepper
20 tiny dill sprigs to garnish

Cut each scone in half. Combine cream and horseradish sauce. Top each scone half with an equal amount of mixture. Cut smoked trout slices into 20 - 1in (2.5cm) wide strips. Top each prepared half with a smoked trout strip and a sprinkle of pepper. Garnish with dill sprigs. Serve at room temperature.

THINK AHEAD
Top scones up to 45 minutes in advance. Garnish just before serving.

TINY CREAM TEA SCONES WITH RASPBERRY PRESERVES

MAKES 20
1 recipe tiny scones (see above)
½ cup (125ml) raspberry preserves
½ cup (125ml) heavy cream

Cut each scone in half. Whip cream until it holds soft peaks (see page 144). Top each scone half with 1 tsp each preserves and cream. Serve at room temperature.

THINK AHEAD
Top scones up to 30 minutes in advance.

TINY HEART SHORTCAKES WITH STRAWBERRIES

MAKES 20
1 recipe tiny heart-shaped scones (see above)
½ cup (125ml) heavy cream
2 tbsp sugar
10 strawberries, halved
2 tsp powered sugar for dusting

ESSENTIAL EQUIPMENT
Piping bag with a large star nozzle

Cut each scone in half. Whip cream until it holds stiff peaks. Beat in the sugar (see page 144). Fill piping bag with cream. Pipe 3 small rosettes onto each scone half (see page 146). Arrange strawberry on top. Dust with powdered sugar. Serve at room temperature.

THINK AHEAD
Top scones up to 30 minutes in advance.

MINI PISSALADIERE

MAKES 24

1 recipe unbaked shortcrust pastry
(see page 136)
1 tbsp olive oil
1 garlic clove, crushed
2 large spanish onions, finely sliced
¾ cup (200ml) tomato passata
1 tsp dried oregano
salt, black pepper
1 tbsp parmesan cheese, grated
24 pitted black olives
6 anchovies, halved lengthwise

ESSENTIAL EQUIPMENT
14in x 10in (35cm x 25cm) jelly roll pan

Preheat oven to 400°F (200°C).
Grease the jelly roll pan. Roll out pastry
on a floured surface to fit the pan. Place
pastry on the pan. Heat oil in a frying
pan over medium heat. Add garlic and
onions and cook until soft, 10 minutes.
Add tomato passata and continue cooking
for 5 minutes. Add oregano and salt and
pepper to taste. Spread onion mixture
over pastry. Bake for 15 minutes. Remove
from oven and sprinkle with parmesan.
Allow to cool in pan; then cut into 24
squares, 2in x 2in (5cm x 5cm).
Cut anchovy pieces in half crosswise. Top
each square with 2 anchovy pieces in a
criss-cross pattern with an olive in the
center. Remove from pan and serve at
room temperature.

THINK AHEAD
Make, cut, and garnish, but leave in pan up to 2 days in
advance. Store in pan covered in the refrigerator. Crisp
in preheated 400°F (200°C) oven for 10 minutes.
Remove from pan before serving.

EGGPLANT AND PINE NUT PIZZETTE

MAKES 20

1 recipe unbaked bread dough
(see page 140)
1 medium eggplant
1 tbsp olive oil
1 garlic clove, crushed
2 tbsp finely chopped parsley
½ cup (125ml) tomato passata
4 tbsp parmesan cheese, grated
3 tbsp pine nuts
salt and black pepper

ESSENTIAL EQUIPMENT
2in (5cm) plain pastry cutter

Preheat oven to 400°F (200°C).
Roll out dough on a floured surface to a
⅛in (0.25cm) thickness. Cut out 20
rounds with the pastry cutter and place
on a floured baking sheet.
Cut eggplant in half lengthwise, then cut
halves into ¼in (0.5cm) thick slices.
Heat oil in a frying pan and add
eggplant, garlic, and parsley. Stir fry
over high heat until wilted, 5 minutes.
Spread each pizzette with 1 tsp tomato
passata. Arrange eggplant slices on top.
Sprinkle with parmesan, pine nuts, salt,
and pepper. Bake until crisp and golden,
10 minutes. Serve warm.

THINK AHEAD
Make up to 1 day in advance. Cover and refrigerate.
Crisp in preheated 400°F (200°G) oven for
10 minutes before serving.

TOMATO AND BASIL PIZZETTE

MAKES 20

1 recipe unbaked bread dough
(see page 140)
½ cup (125ml) tomato passata
¾ cup (15g) basil leaves
4oz (125g) mozzarella cheese, finely sliced
4 tbsp parmesan cheese, grated
salt, black pepper

ESSENTIAL EQUIPMENT
2in (5cm) plain pastry cutter

Preheat oven to 400°F (200°C).
Roll dough out on a floured surface to a
⅛in (0.25cm) thickness. Cut out 20
rounds with the pastry cutter and place
on a floured baking sheet.
Cut mozzarella slices into 20 equal-sized
pieces. Spread each round with 1 tsp
tomato passata and arrange over 2 basil
leaves. Place a piece of mozzarella on
top. Sprinkle with parmesan, salt, and
pepper. Bake until crisp and golden, 10
minutes. Serve warm.

THINK AHEAD
Make up to 1 day in advance. Cover and refrigerate.
Crisp in preheated 400°F (200°C) oven for
10 minutes before serving.

MINI APPLE TATINS

MAKES 20

¼ of a 14oz package (100g) puff pastry
⅓ cup (100g) sugar
2 tbsp water
2½ apples, quartered and cored
2 tsp powdered sugar for dusting

ESSENTIAL EQUIPMENT
2 -12-cup mini muffin pans, 2in (5cm) plain pastry cutter

Preheat oven 400°F (200°C).
Roll out pastry on a floured surface to a ¼in (0.5cm) thickness. Cut out 20 rounds with the pastry cutter.
Put sugar and water in a small pan. Stir to dissolve; then place over medium heat and bring to a boil. Cook to a dark caramel (see page 145). Divide caramel evenly among 20 of the cups of the muffin pans.
Cut each apple quarter across into 6 slices, about ¼in (0.5cm) thick. Arrange 3 apple pieces over the caramel in each cup. Press pastry rounds on top. Bake until pastry is crisp and golden, 10 minutes. Cool slightly before turning out. Dust with powdered sugar. Serve warm.

THINK AHEAD
Bake up to 1 day in advance, but do not turn out of pans. Store covered at room temperature. Reheat in preheated 400°F (200°G) oven for 10 minutes. Finish as directed.

COOKS' NOTE
In France, Golden Delicious apples are traditionally used for making tarte tatin. This is because they retain their shape well and do not disintegrate when baked. Granny Smith or Cox apples, however, also produce good results.

MINI RED ONION TATINS

MAKES 20

2 red onions
2 tsp finely chopped thyme
salt, black pepper
1 tbsp olive oil
¼ of a 14oz package (100g) puff pastry
⅓ cup (100g) sugar
2 tbsp water
1 tbsp balsamic vinegar
3 thyme sprigs, roughly chopped, to garnish

ESSENTIAL EQUIPMENT
2 - 12-cup mini muffin pans, 2in (5cm) plain pastry cutter

Preheat oven to 400°F (200°C). Cut each onion quarter across into 5 pieces, about ¼in (0.5cm) each. Place pieces on a greased baking sheet. Sprinkle with chopped thyme, salt, pepper, and oil. Bake for 10 minutes.
Meanwhile, roll out pastry on a floured surface to a ¼in (0.5cm) thickness. Cut out 20 rounds with the pastry cutter. Put sugar and water in a small pan and stir to dissolve. Place over medium heat and bring to a boil. Cook to a dark caramel (see page 145). Divide caramel evenly among 20 of the muffin cups. Arrange 2 onion pieces over the caramel in each muffin cup. Press pastry rounds on top. Bake until pastry is crisp and golden, 10 minutes. Cool slightly before turning out. Sprinkle with thyme and drizzle with vinegar. Serve warm.

THINK AHEAD
Bake up to 1 day in advance, but do not turn out of tins. Store covered at room temperature. Reheat in preheated 400°F (200°C) oven for 5 minutes. Turn out and finish as directed.

CANAPES

MAKES 20
7 thin slices bread

SPECIAL EQUIPMENT
2in (5cm) fluted pastry cutter

Cut bread slices into 20 rounds with the pastry cutter.

THINK AHEAD
Prepare up to 1 day in advance. Store in an airtight container.

COOKS' NOTE
We urge you to look beyond white and brown bread for canapé bases; the wealth of specialty breads now available offer a short-cut to simple but flavorsome canapés. Also try using different shaped cutters - another easy but surefire way to add instant appeal.

GRAVLAX ON PUMPERNICKEL CANAPES WITH DILL-MUSTARD SAUCE

MAKES 20
1½ tsp white wine vinegar
2 tsp sugar
2 tbsp dijon mustard
1 tbsp finely chopped dill
1 tsp white pepper
2½ tbsp sunflower oil
5 pumpernickel slices
10oz (300g) gravlax slices

For sauce, combine vinegar, sugar, mustard, dill, and pepper; whisk in oil until thick and creamy. Lay gravlax on the pumpernickel slices. Cut each pumpernickel and gravlax slice into 20 - 1in (2.5cm) wide strips. Drizzle with sauce. Serve chilled or at room temperature.

THINK AHEAD
Assemble up to 3 hours in advance. Cover tightly with plastic wrap and refrigerate. Drizzle with sauce up to 1 hour before serving.

VALENTINE CUCUMBER CREAM CANAPES

MAKES 20
½ cucumber
8oz (200g) package cream cheese
10 thin white bread slices
3 tbsp finely chopped parsley
salt, white pepper

ESSENTIAL EQUIPMENT
1½ in (3.5cm) heart-shaped pastry cutter
2½ in (6cm) heart-shaped pastry cutter

Cut cucumber into ¼in (0.5cm) slices. With the smaller cutter, cut out 20 hearts . Spread cream cheese on bread. Cut out 20 hearts with larger pastry cutter. Put parsley on small dish. Dip edges of canapés in parsley. Top canapés with cucumber hearts and sprinkle with salt and pepper. Serve chilled or at room temperature.

THINK AHEAD
Assemble up to 3 hours in advance. Cover tightly with plastic wrap and refrigerate.

SMOKED OYSTERS ON RYE CANAPES WITH SOUR CREAM AND TARRAGON

MAKES 20
20 drained smoked oysters
⅔ cup (150ml) sour cream
1 recipe rye canapé bases (see page 52)
salt, black pepper
20 tarragon sprigs to garnish

Pat oysters dry with paper towels. Divide sour cream evenly among canapé bases. Place oyster on top and sprinkle with salt and pepper. Garnish with tarragon. Serve chilled or at room temperature.

THINK AHEAD
Top canapés up to 45 minutes in advance.

PARIS HAM WITH DIJON BUTTER CANAPES

MAKES 20
6 tbsp (90g) butter, softened
1 tsp dijon mustard
1 recipe white bread canapé bases (see page 52)
½lb (200g) ham, thickly sliced
20 cornichon fans to garnish (see below)
ESSENTIAL EQUIPMENT
2in (5cm) fluted pastry cutter

Mix butter and mustard. Spread on canapé bases. Cut out 20 rounds of ham with pastry cutter. Fold each ham round in half and place on canapés. Garnish with cornichon fans. Serve chilled or at room temperature.

THINK AHEAD
Top canapés up to 3 hours in advance. Cover tightly with plastic wrap and refrigerate.

CARPACCIO CANAPES

MAKES 20
1 tbsp mayonnaise (see page 142)
dash of worcestershire sauce
squeeze of lemon juice
1 tbsp milk
salt, white pepper
¼lb (100g) beef fillet steak, 1in (2.5cm) thick
1 recipe brown bread canapé bases (see page 52)
ESSENTIAL EQUIPMENT
paper piping cone (see page 146)

Combine mayonnaise, worcestershire sauce, lemon, and milk. Add salt and pepper to taste. Cut steak across the grain into 2in (5cm) wide strips. Place strips end to end in a line on top of a piece of foil. Roll beef strips up tightly in the foil. Twist the ends of foil to give the beef strips a rounded shape. Chill for 20 minutes in freezer. Cut beef into ⅛in (0.25cm) slices (see below, left). Flatten each slice by setting the blade of the knife on top and pressing down lightly. Divide beef slices among canapé bases. Fill paper piping cone with sauce. Pipe over sauce. Serve at room temperature.

THINK AHEAD
Make sauce up to 1 day in advance. Cover and refrigerate. Roll beef up to 1 day in advance; refrigerate. Top canapés up to 45 minutes in advance.

COOKS' NOTE
If you don't feel comfortable serving raw beef, rare roast beef slices can be used as an alternative. Use a 2in (5cm) pastry cutter to cut the roast beef into rounds. Top canapés and drizzle over sauce.

CORNICHON FANS
Cut 10 cornichons in half lengthwise. Cut fine slices through each cornichon half, leaving slices attached at one end.

BEET ROSTI WITH SMOKED TROUT AND HORSERADISH MOUSSE

MAKES 20

FOR MOUSSE
⅓lb (150g) smoked trout
½ of 8oz (125g) package cream cheese
1 tbsp horseradish sauce
1 tbsp lemon juice
cayenne pepper

ESSENTIAL EQUIPMENT
9in (23cm) non-stick frying pan, 1¾ in (4.5cm) fluted pastry cutter, piping bag with a large star nozzle

FOR ROSTI
¾ cup (250g) cooked beets, grated
1 large potato, grated and squeezed dry
1 tbsp all-purpose flour
1 egg, beaten
¾ tsp salt, ¼ tsp black pepper
2 tbsp sunflower oil
paprika to garnish

For mousse, place trout, cream cheese, horseradish, and lemon in a food processor or blender; pulse to a smooth paste. Add cayenne pepper to taste.

For rosti, mix beets, potato, flour, egg, salt and pepper together. Heat 1 tbsp oil in a non-stick pan. Spread half the potato mixture, ¼in (0.5cm) thick, across the bottom of the pan. Reduce heat to low and cook until both sides are crisp and golden, about 10 minutes per side. Remove from pan and cool slightly on paper towels. Heat the remaining oil. Cook and cool the remaining potato mixture. Cut out 10 rounds from each rosti with the pastry cutter (see opposite, middle). Cool completely before topping. Fill piping bag with mousse and pipe onto rostis (see page 146). Sprinkle with paprika to garnish. Serve at room temperature.

THINK AHEAD
Make mousse up to 3 days in advance. Cover and refrigerate. Make rosti rounds up to 2 days in advance. Store in layers on waxed paper in an airtight container in the refrigerator. Crisp in preheated 400°F (200°C) oven for 5 minutes. Top and garnish up to 1 hour before serving.

Stamp out rounds from each rosti.

POTATO ROSTI WITH CREME FRAICHE, CAVIAR AND DILL

MAKES 20
1lb (500g) potatoes, grated and squeezed dry
1 tsp flour
¾ tsp salt, ¼ tsp black pepper
2 tbsp sunflower oil
½ cup (125ml) crème fraîche
3½ oz (100g) black lumpfish caviar
20 dill sprigs to garnish

ESSENTIAL EQUIPMENT
9in (23cm) non-stick frying pan, 1¾ in (4.5cm) plain pastry cutter

Mix potato, flour, salt, and pepper together. Heat 1 tbsp oil in the non-stick pan. Spread half the potato mixture, ¼in (0.5cm) thick, across the bottom of the pan. Reduce heat to low and cook until both sides are crisp and golden, about 10 minutes per side. Remove from pan and cool slightly on paper towels. Heat the remaining oil. Cook and cool the remaining potato mixture.
Cut out 10 rounds from each rosti with the pastry cutter (see opposite, middle). Cool completely before topping. Top mini rostis with 1 tsp each crème fraîche and caviar. Garnish with dill sprigs. Serve warm.

THINK AHEAD
Make rosti rounds up to 2 days in advance. Store in layers on waxed paper in an airtight container in the refrigerator. Crisp in preheated 400°F (200°C) oven for 5 minutes. Top up to 45 minutes before serving.

MINI LATKES WITH SOUR CREAM AND APPLE SAUCE

MAKES 20

1lb (500g) potatoes, grated
and squeezed dry
1 onion, grated and squeezed dry
1 tbsp all-purpose flour
1 egg, beaten
¾ tsp salt, ¼ tsp black pepper
2 tbsp sunflower oil
½ cup (125ml) sour cream
½ cup (125ml) apple sauce
2 tbsp finely chopped chives

Mix potatoes, onion, flour, egg, salt, and
pepper together. Heat oil in a frying pan
over medium heat. Working in batches,
drop heaped teaspoonfuls of mixture
into the hot oil. Use the back of spoon
to flatten them into thin pancakes.
Cook, turning once, until crisp and
golden on each side. Drain on paper
towels. Cool slightly before topping.
Top latkes with 1 tsp each sour cream
and apple sauce. Garnish with chopped
chives. Serve warm or at room
temperature.

THINK AHEAD
Make latkes up to 2 days in advance. Store in layers on
waxed paper in an airtight container in the refrigerator. Crisp in preheated 400°F (200°C) oven for 5 minutes. Top up to 45 minutes before serving.

COOKS' NOTE
The oaken, salty flavor of smoked fish perfectly
complements these crispy potato pancakes. Try the
classic combination of smoked salmon, sour cream,
and a squeeze of lemon.

CRISPY CARROT AND SCALLION CAKES WITH FETA AND BLACK OLIVE

MAKES 20

1½ cups (250g) carrots, grated
1 cup (250g) potatoes, grated and
squeezed dry
2 scallions, finely chopped
1 tbsp all-purpose flour
1 egg, beaten
¾ tsp salt, ¼ tsp black pepper
2 tbsp sunflower oil
¾ cup (100g) feta cheese, crumbled
10 pitted black olives, quartered

Mix carrot, potato, scallions, flour, egg,
and salt and pepper together. Heat oil in
a frying pan over medium heat.
Working in batches, drop heaped
teaspoonfuls of mixture into the hot oil.
Use the back of the spoon to flatten
them into thin pancakes. Cook, turning
once, until crisp and golden on each
side, 5 minutes per side. Drain on paper
towels. Cool to room temperature before
topping. Divide feta cheese and olives
among the cakes. Serve at room
temperature.

THINK AHEAD
Make up to 2 days in advance. Store in layers on paper
towels in an airtight container at room temperature.
Crisp in 400°F (200°C) oven for 3 minutes. Top 45 minutes before serving.

BABY BAKED POTATOES WITH SOUR CREAM AND CAVIAR

MAKES 20

20 tiny new potatoes, (about ¾in diameter)
pricked with a fork
1 tbsp olive oil
2 tsp salt
½ cup (125ml) sour cream
3½ oz (100g) black lumpfish caviar

Preheat oven to 400°F (200°C).
Toss potatoes with oil and salt until
evenly coated. Place on a baking sheet
and cook until soft inside and crisp
outside, about 30 minutes. Cool completely. Cut a cross on top of each potato and squeeze gently to open.
Top each tiny potato with 1 tsp each
sour cream and caviar. Serve at once.

THINK AHEAD
Bake potatoes up to 1 day in advance. Store in an
airtight container in the refrigerator. Crisp in preheated 400°F (200°C) oven for 5 minutes. Top just before
serving.

KIWI AND PASSIONFRUIT MINI PAVLOVAS

MAKES 20

1 recipe baked vanilla mini meringues
(see page 141)
⅓ cup (75ml) whipping cream
1 tbsp granulated sugar
1 kiwi
2 passion fruit, halved
20 raspberries
2 tsp powdered sugar for dusting

Whip cream until it holds soft peaks.
Mix in granulated sugar (see page 144).
Cut kiwi in half and cut each half into 5
slices. Cut each slice in half. Scoop out
pulp from passion fruit halves. Top each
pavlova with 1 tsp cream. Arrange a half
kiwi slice and a raspberry on top. Spoon
over passion fruit and dust with powdered sugar.

THINK AHEAD
Assemble meringues up to 3 hours in advance; store
at room temperature.

MUSCOVADO AND FIG MINI MERINGUES

MAKES 20

1 recipe baked muscovado mini meringues
(see page 141)
2 figs
2oz (60g) plain chocolate, melted
(see page 145)
½ cup (125ml) crème fraîche
2 tsp cocoa powder for dusting

Cut figs in half, then slice each half into
5 slivers. Top individual meringues with
1 tsp crème fraîche and dust lightly with
cocoa powder. Arrange 1 fig sliver on
top and, using a teaspoon, drizzle with
melted chocolate. Serve at room
temperature.

THINK AHEAD
Assemble meringues up to 3 hours in advance; store
at room temperature.

STRAWBERRY AND PISTACHIO MINI MERINGUES

MAKES 20

1 recipe baked pistachio mini meringues
(see page 141)
5 strawberries
⅓ cup (75ml) whipping cream
1 tbsp granulated sugar
2 tsp powdered sugar for dusting
2 tbsp chopped pistachios to garnish

Cut strawberries into quarters. Whip
cream until it holds soft peaks. Mix in
granulated sugar (see page 144). Top
each meringue with 1 tsp cream and
dust with powdered sugar. Arrange
strawberry quarters on top. Garnish
with chopped pistachios.

THINK AHEAD
Assemble meringues 3 hours before serving; store at
room temperature.

HAZELNUT AND RASPBERRY MINI MERINGUES

MAKES 20

1 recipe baked hazelnut mini meringues
(see page 141)
⅓ cup (75ml) whipping cream
1 tbsp sugar
2 cups (250g) raspberries
2 tsp powdered sugar for dusting
20 tiny mint sprigs to garnish

Whip cream until it holds soft peaks.
Mix in sugar (see page 144). Top each
pavlova with 1 tsp cream. Arrange
raspberries on top and dust with powdered sugar. Garnish with mint sprigs.

THINK AHEAD
Assemble meringues up to 3 hours in advance; store
at room temperature.

POLENTA CROSTINI

MAKES 20

3 cups (850ml) water
1 cup (175g) instant polenta
1 tsp salt
4 tbsp grated parmesan cheese
½ tsp black pepper
2 tbsp olive oil

ESSENTIAL EQUIPMENT
1lb (500g) greased loaf pan

Bring water to a boil in a large pan. Stir in the polenta and salt. Cook, stirring constantly, until thick, 5-10 minutes. Add parmesan and pepper. Pour hot polenta into the greased loaf pan (see below). After cooling completely, unmold from the pan. Slice into 10 slices (see below); then cut each slice diagonally into 2 triangles. Place triangles on greased baking sheets. Brush with oil. Toast under a preheated broiler until lightly golden and crisp, 3 minutes. Cool to room temperature before topping.

THINK AHEAD
Make polenta up to 3 days in advance, leaving it in the pan. Cover and refrigerate. Cut and broil it up to 2 hours in advance. Store at room temperature.

COOKS' NOTE
Add 2 crushed garlic cloves and 1 tbsp finely chopped herbs - rosemary, thyme, or oregano - to the cooked, hot polenta for a little extra flavour.

Pour into an oiled loaf pan.

Unmold polenta from the pan and slice.

POLENTA CROSTINI WITH BLUE CHEESE AND BALSAMIC RED ONIONS

MAKES 20

2 tbsp olive oil
2 medium red onions, sliced
½ tsp salt
1 tbsp balsamic vinegar
black pepper
1 recipe polenta crostini (see opposite)
1 cup (125g) dolcelatte or danish blue cheese, crumbled

Heat oil in a pan over medium heat. Add onions and salt. Cook, stirring occasionally, until soft and tender, 10 minutes. Add vinegar and cook until evaporated, 3 minutes. Add pepper to taste. Cool to room temperature. Divide onions evenly among crostini; then top each one with 1 tsp crumbled cheese. Serve at room temperature.

THINK AHEAD
Cook onions up to 1 day in advance. Cover and store at room temperature. Top crostini 1 hour in advance. Store at room temperature.

POLENTA CROSTINI WITH TOMATO AND BLACK OLIVE SALSA

MAKES 20

2 ripe tomatoes, peeled, seeded and diced (see page 147)
1 medium red onion, finely chopped
¼ cup (45g) pitted black olives, finely chopped
2 tsp olive oil
1 tsp red wine vinegar
salt, pepper
1 recipe polenta crostini (see opposite)

Combine tomatoes, onion, olives, oil, and vinegar. Add salt and pepper to taste. Cover and let stand at room temperature for 30 minutes to allow the flavors to blend.
Top polenta crostini with salsa. Serve at room temperature.

THINK AHEAD
Make salsa up to 1 day in advance but do not add salt and pepper until just before using. Store in an airtight container in the refrigerator. Top crostini 1 hour in advance. Store at room temperature.

TOSTADITAS

MAKES 24

3 - 6in (15cm) flour tortillas
½ tbsp sunflower oil
¼ tsp salt

Preheat oven to 400°F (200°C).
Brush tortillas on one side with oil.
Cut each tortilla into 8 even-sized
wedges with kitchen scissors or a
serrated knife. Arrange oiled side up
in a single layer on a greased baking
sheet. Sprinkle with salt. Bake until
crisp, 5-7 minutes. Cool on a wire
rack.

THINK AHEAD
Make tostaditas up to 5 days in advance. Store in
an airtight container at room temperature.

COOKS' NOTE
Good-quality store-bought corn chips can be
used as a time-saving alternative. Be sure to buy
plain, lightly salted chips, not ones that are flavored with spices. A flavored chip won't allow
you to appreciate the delicious topping.

TOSTADITAS WITH ROAST CORN SALSA

MAKES 24
½ corn on the cob
½ red pepper, seeded and quartered
½ green chili, seeded and finely chopped
½ medium red onion, finely chopped
1 tbsp finely chopped cilantro
1 tbsp lime juice
1 tbsp olive oil
salt, black pepper
1 recipe tostaditas (see opposite)

Preheat oven to 350°F (180°C).
Rinse corn under cold water to moisten. Place corn and pepper quarters on a baking
pan. Roast for 25 minutes. Remove pepper. Peel and seed (see page 147). Roast
corn for a further 20 minutes.
Finely dice the pepper. When corn is cool, cut the roasted kernels from the cob with
a sharp knife. Combine corn, peppers, chili, onion, cilantro, lime, and oil. Add salt
and pepper to taste. Cover and refrigerate for 1 hour to allow flavors to blend. Top
tostaditas with salsa. Serve chilled or at room temperature.

THINK AHEAD
Make salsa up to 1 day in advance, but do not add the cilantro more than 3 hours before serving. Cover and
refrigerate. Top tostaditas and serve immediately.

COOKS' NOTE
Oven roasting the corn is an important step because it allows the natural sugar in the corn to caramelize. It
also adds a nutty, smoky flavor to the corn's natural sweetness.

TOSTADITAS WITH CITRUS CEVICHE

MAKES 24

¼lb (125g) halibut fillet
juice of 1 lime
juice of ½ lemon
2 tbsp orange juice
1 red chili, seeded and finely chopped
1 scallion, white stem only, finely chopped
1 tomato, seeded and diced (see page 147)
1 small avocado, diced
2 tbsp finely chopped cilantro
½ tsp salt
1 recipe tostaditas (see page 59)
cilantro leaves to garnish

Finely dice the fish. Combine fish with the lime, lemon, and orange juices in a non-metallic bowl. Cover and refrigerate for 3 hours, stirring occasionally. Drain fish well, discarding all but 1 tbsp marinade. Toss the fish, chili, tomato, scallion, onion, avocado, cilantro, and reserved 1 tbsp marinade together to combine. Top tostaditas with equal amounts of the ceviche. Serve chilled.

THINK AHEAD
Make ceviche up to 1 day in advance, but do not add the avocado and cilantro more than 3 hours before serving. Press plastic wrap tightly over the surface of the ceviche and refrigerate. Top tostaditas just before serving.

COOKS' NOTE
Fresh tuna, salmon, or scallops also make excellent ceviche. Use cooked shrimp if you prefer not to use raw fish.

TOSTADITAS WITH BLACKENED SNAPPER, PEACH RELISH, AND SOUR CREAM

MAKES 24

¼ tsp dried thyme
¼ tsp dried oregano
¼ tsp paprika
¼ tsp cumin seeds
¼ tsp garlic powder
½ tsp salt, ¼ tsp black pepper
¼lb (125g) red snapper fillet, ½in (1cm) thick
2 tsp sunflower oil
1 pitted peach, fresh or canned, finely diced
2 tsp lemon juice
1 recipe tostaditas (see page 59)
5 tbsp sour cream to garnish

Combine thyme, oregano, paprika, cumin, garlic, salt, and pepper on a plate. Cut fish into 24 - ½in (1cm) cubes. Dip fish in oil, then roll in spice mixture. Preheat a dry frying pan over medium heat until very hot. Add fish cubes, spiced side down. Cook cubes 2 minutes per side until firm to the touch. Remove from pan and cool.
For relish, combine peach and lemon juice. Divide relish evenly among tostaditas. Top with fish. Garnish with sour cream. Serve chilled or at room temperature.

THINK AHEAD
Cook fish up to 1 day in advance. Cover and refrigerate. Make relish up to 1 day in advance. Cover and refrigerate. Top tostaditas up to 45 minutes before serving.

MINI PAPADUMS WITH CREAMY CHICKEN TIKKA

MAKES 30

30 mini papadum
1 tbsp sunflower oil
1 boneless, skinless chicken breast half
1in (2.5cm) fresh ginger, grated
1 garlic clove, crushed
½ tsp ground cardamon
½ tsp ground cumin
½ tsp salt, ¼ tsp black pepper
1 tbsp lemon juice
4 tbsp whole-milk yogurt
½ tsp paprika for sprinkling
20 cilantro leaves to garnish

Preheat oven to 400°F (200°C). Place mini papadums in a single layer on a greased baking sheet. Brush with oil. Bake until crisp and golden, 3-5 minutes. Cool on a wire rack. Cut chicken into ¼in (0.5cm) thick slices. Combine chicken, ginger, garlic, spices, salt, pepper, lemon, and yogurt in a non-metallic bowl. Cover and refrigerate for at least 1 hour. Place chicken under a preheated broiler until cooked through, 8-10 minutes. Cool. Roughly chop. Divide chicken evenly among the papadums. Sprinkle with paprika and garnish with cilantro. Serve chilled or at room temperature.

THINK AHEAD
Bake papadums up to 2 days in advance. Store in an airtight container at room temperature. Marinate chicken up to 1 day in advance. Cook chicken up to 1 day in advance. Cover and refrigerate. Top papadums up to 1 hour before serving.

COOKS' NOTE
Look for mini papadums at gourmet food stores and Indian markets. If you have difficulty finding them, this Indian-inspired topping is also delicious served on tostaditas.

GINGERED CHICKEN CAKES WITH CILANTRO-LIME MAYONNAISE

MAKES 20

FOR CAKES

2 boneless, skinless chicken breast halves
2 tbsp fish sauce
1in (2.5cm) fresh ginger, roughly chopped
3 scallions, roughly chopped
1 garlic clove, crushed
1 tsp salt, ¼ tsp tabasco

FOR TOPPING

4 tbsp mayonnaise (see page 142)
½ cup (15g) cilantro, finely chopped
juice of 1 lime
2 tbsp diced mango (see page 163) to garnish

Preheat oven to 400°F (200°C).
For cakes, place all cake ingredients in a food processor or blender; pulse until finely minced. Divide mixture into 20 walnut-sized pieces. With wet hands, shape each piece into a ball and flatten into a cake. Place cakes on a greased baking sheet and cook until golden and cooked through, 12 minutes. Cool to warm or room temperature.
For topping, combine mayonnaise, cilantro, and lime. Spoon topping onto cakes. Garnish with diced mango. Serve warm or at room temperature.

THINK AHEAD
Assemble cakes and prepare topping up to 1 day in advance. Cover and refrigerate. Bake and top cakes up to 1 hour in advance. Keep at room temperature. Garnish and serve.

COOKS' NOTE
Try using pork fillet instead of chicken and lemon grass instead of ginger for a tasty variation on these asian-inspired cakes.

COCKTAIL SALMON AND DILL CAKES WITH CREME FRAICHE TARTARE

MAKES 20

FOR CAKES

⅓lb (150g) salmon fillet
1 large potato
2 tbsp roughly chopped dill
2 tbsp tomato ketchup
1 tsp horseradish sauce
1 tsp lemon juice
1 tsp salt, ¼ tsp tabasco
2 tbsp fresh breadcrumbs

FOR TOPPING

4 tbsp crème fraîche
1 tsp drained capers, finely chopped
1 tsp drained cocktail gherkins, finely chopped
1 tsp finely chopped tarragon
salt, black pepper
20 watercress sprigs to garnish

Place salmon in pan of boiling water. Return the water to a boil; then remove pan from heat at once. Cool thoroughly. Drain on paper towels. Separate cooked salmon into large flakes.
Preheat oven to 400°F (200°C). Cook potato in boiling water until tender; mash until smooth. Combine potato with salmon, dill, ketchup, horseradish sauce, and lemon. Add salt and pepper to taste. Divide mixture into 20 walnut-sized pieces. Shape pieces into balls and roll in breadcrumbs. Flatten into cakes and place on a greased baking sheet. Bake until golden, 10 minutes. Cool to warm or room temperature.
For topping, combine all topping ingredients. Add salt and pepper to taste. Spoon topping onto cakes. Garnish with watercress. Serve warm or at room temperature.

THINK AHEAD
Assemble cakes and prepare topping up to 1 day in advance. Cover and refrigerate. Bake and top cakes up to 1 hour in advance. Store at room temperature. Garnish just before serving.

MINI DEVILED CRAB CAKES WITH TOMATO REMOULADE

MAKES 20

FOR CAKES
½lb (250g) crab meat
½ onion, finely chopped
½ tsp honey
½ tsp dry mustard
½ tsp tabasco
1 tsp horseradish sauce
1 tsp worcestershire sauce
1 tsp lemon juice
3 tbsp mayonnaise (see page 142)
½ cup fresh breadcrumbs
salt, black pepper

FOR TOPPING
4 tbsp mayonnaise (see page 142)
2 tsp finely chopped chives
1 tsp lemon juice
½ tsp dijon mustard
½ tsp garlic, finely chopped
salt, black pepper
1 tomato, peeled, seeded, chopped, and diced, to garnish (see page 147)

For cakes, mix crab, onion, honey, dry mustard, tabasco, horseradish, and worcestershire sauces, lemon juice, and mayonnaise together. Add enough fresh breadcrumbs to bind, about 2-4 tbsp. Add salt and pepper to taste. Divide mixture into heaped teaspoonfuls, about 20 walnut-sized pieces. Shape each piece into a ball and roll lightly in remaining crumbs. Place on a greased baking sheet. Refrigerate until firm, 30 minutes. Preheat oven to 400°F (200°C). Bake crab cakes until crisp and golden, 10 minutes. Cool to warm or room temperature.
For topping, combine mayonnaise, chives, lemon juice, mustard, and garlic. Add salt and pepper to taste. Spoon topping onto crab cakes. Garnish with tomato. Serve warm or at room temperature.

THINK AHEAD
Assemble cakes and make topping up to 1 day in advance. Cover and refrigerate. Bake and top cakes up to 1 hour before serving.

EGGPLANT AND PINE NUT FRITTERS WITH ROASTED TOMATOES

MAKES 20

FOR TOPPING
2 plum tomatoes, halved
1 garlic clove, sliced
1 tsp balsamic vinegar
½ tsp honey
½ tsp finely chopped rosemary
salt, black pepper

FOR FRITTERS
2 tbsp olive oil
1 medium eggplant, diced
1 garlic clove, crushed
1 tbsp finely chopped parsley
1 tsp finely chopped rosemary
1 egg plus 1 egg yolk, beaten
¾ cup (75g) parmesan cheese, grated
1 cup (100g) mozzarella cheese, diced
1 cup (60g) dry breadcrumbs
½ cup (60g) pine nuts, roughly chopped
salt, black pepper
20 small arugula leaves to garnish

Preheat oven to 400°F (200°C).
For topping, put tomatoes and garlic in a baking pan. Drizzle with vinegar and honey and sprinkle with rosemary, salt, and pepper. Roast in oven until softened, 20 minutes. Cool and place in a food processor or blender; pulse until smooth. For fritters, heat oil in a skillet over medium-high heat. Stir fry diced eggplant until soft and golden, 10 minutes. Drain and cool on paper towels. Combine with garlic, parsley, rosemary, beaten eggs, parmesan, mozzarella, breadcrumbs, and pine nuts. Add salt and pepper to taste. Divide mixture into 20 walnut-sized pieces. Shape each piece into an oval. Place ovals on a greased baking sheet. Bake until golden, 10 minutes. Cool to warm or room temperature. Spoon topping onto cakes. Garnish with arugula. Serve warm or at room temperature.

THINK AHEAD
Assemble fritters and prepare topping up to 1 day in advance. Cover and refrigerate. Cook and top fritters up to 1 hour in advance. Store at room temperature. Garnish just before serving.

MINI STICKY ORANGE AND ALMOND CAKES

MAKES 25

2 oranges
6 eggs, beaten
1 cup (250g) sugar
2 cups (250g) ground almonds
1 tsp baking powder
⅔ cup (150ml) whole-milk yogurt
4 tbsp pomegranate seeds (see below)
to garnish

ESSENTIAL EQUIPMENT
14 x 10in (35 x 25cm) jelly roll pan lined with buttered baking parchment,
¾ in (4.25cm) pastry cutter

Cook the whole peeled oranges in boiling water until soft, 1½ hours. Cool thoroughly. Preheat oven to 375°F (190°C).
For cake, cut oranges in half and remove any seeds. Place in a food processor; process to a smooth purée. Add eggs, sugar, almonds, and baking powder; pulse until well blended. Pour batter into the lined pan. Bake until firm to the touch, 40 minutes. Cool completely. Cut pomegranate in half through the middle of the stem end. Cut each half into quarters (see below, top right). Pull stem ends of each quarter toward each other, bending peel back to release pomegranate seeds (see below, bottom right). Cut cake into 20 rounds with the pastry cutter (see below, left). Spoon ½ tsp yogurt onto each cake round. Garnish with pomegranate seeds. Serve at room temperature.

THINK AHEAD
Make cake up to 2 days in advance. Store at room temperature. Alternatively, bake and freeze cake up to 1 month in advance (see page 149). Defrost in the refrigerator overnight. Glaze cakes up to 3 hours ahead. Leave at room temperature, until ready to serve.

Stamp out cake rounds.

Cut pomegranate into quarters.

Pull back peel to release kernels.

MINI CHOCOLATE TRUFFLE CAKES

MAKES 25

FOR CAKE
14oz (400g) dark chocolate, broken into pieces
⅔ cup (150g) butter
⅔ cup (150g) sugar
5 eggs, separated
⅓ cup (45g) all-purpose flour

FOR GLAZE
2½ oz (75g) dark chocolate, broken into pieces
5 tbsp heavy cream

ESSENTIAL EQUIPMENT
14 x 10in (35 x 25cm) jelly roll pan lined with buttered baking parchment,
1¾in (4.25cm) pastry cutter

Preheat oven to 300°F (150°C).
For cake, melt butter and chocolate together in a double boiler over low heat. Stir continuously until smooth and melted. Remove from heat and cool to lukewarm. Beat sugar, egg yolks, and flour into the cool chocolate. Beat egg whites until they hold soft peaks (see page 141). Gently fold chocolate mixture into whites until evenly combined. Pour batter into the lined pan. Bake until firm to the touch, 20 minutes. Cool thoroughly.
For glaze, heat cream in a pan just below the boiling point. Remove from heat. Stir in chocolate until melted and smooth. Cool until slightly thickened, 30 minutes. Cut cooled cake into 20 rounds with the pastry cutter. Spoon 1 heaped teaspoonful glaze over each cake round. Serve at room temperature.

THINK AHEAD
Bake cake up to 5 days in advance. Store at room temperature. Alternatively, bake and freeze cake up to 1 month in advance (see page 149). Defrost in refrigerator overnight. Cut and glaze cake rounds up to 3 hours in advance. Leave at room temperature until ready to serve.

STICKS AND SKEWERS

PROSCIUTTO-WRAPPED SCALLOP BROCHETTES WITH SAUCE BEARNAISE

MAKES 20

20 bay scallops or 10 sea scallops
7 very thin prosciutto slices
20 large basil leaves
salt, black pepper
1 recipe sauce bearnaise (see page 143)

ESSENTIAL EQUIPMENT
20 - 6in (15cm) wooden skewers presoaked in cold water

If using sea scallops, slice in half. Cut prosciutto slices into 3 strips. Place 1 basil leaf on each prosciutto strip and 1 bay scallop or ½ sea scallop on top. Sprinkle with a pinch of both salt and pepper. Wrap basil and prosciutto around each scallop. Secure each wrapped scallop with 1 presoaked skewer.
Preheat broiler. Alternatively, preheat a ridged cast-iron griddle, or a barbecue grill. Broil, grill, or pan-griddle scallop brochettes until scallops have turned from opaque to white, 1-2 minutes on each side. Serve hot, warm, or at room temperature with sauce bearnaise.

THINK AHEAD
Skewer scallops up to 8 hours in advance. Store in an airtight container in the refrigerator.

TANGY THAI SHRIMP SKEWERS

MAKES 20

20 medium shrimp, cooked and peeled
2 garlic cloves, finely chopped
½ in (1cm) piece fresh ginger, grated
1 red chili, seeded and finely chopped
1 tsp granulated sugar
1 tbsp fish sauce
juice of 1 lime

ESSENTIAL EQUIPMENT
20 - 3in (7.5cm) wooden skewers or toothpicks

Pat shrimp dry with paper towels. Combine shrimp, garlic, ginger, chili, sugar, sauce, and lime in a non-metallic bowl. Cover and refrigerate for 1 hour. Skewer 1 shrimp onto each skewer. Serve chilled.

THINK AHEAD
Marinate shrimp up to 6 hours in advance. Skewer shrimp up to 3 hours in advance. Store in an airtight container in the refrigerator.

COOKS' NOTE ON GRILLING WITH SKEWERS

Don't forget to presoak wooden skewers when using them in a recipe calling for broiling or grilling. Soak the skewers for at least 30 minutes in cold water to prevent them from scorching.

BARBECUED TANDOORI SHRIMP STICKS

MAKES 20

½ cup (125ml) whole-milk yogurt
2 tbsp lemon juice
3 garlic cloves, crushed
1in (2.5cm) piece fresh ginger, grated
1 tsp turmeric
1 tsp paprika
¼ tsp ground cardamom
¼ tsp cayenne pepper, 1 tsp salt
20 raw medium shrimp, peeled and deveined (see page 164)

ESSENTIAL EQUIPMENT
20 - 3in (7.5cm) wooden skewers or toothpicks presoaked in cold water

For marinade, combine yogurt, lemon, garlic, ginger, spices, and salt in a non-metallic bowl. Add shrimp and toss in marinade to coat each one well. Cover and refrigerate for 1 hour. Thread 1 shrimp on to each presoaked skewer. Preheat broiler. Alternatively, preheat a ridged cast-iron griddle, grill pan, or barbecue. Broil shrimp until they turn pink and lose their transparency, 3 minutes on each side. Serve hot, warm or at room temperature.

THINK AHEAD
Marinate shrimp up to 4 hours in advance. Store in an airtight container in the refrigerator. Skewer shrimp up to 1 hour in advance. Store in an airtight container in the refrigerator.

GRAPEFRUIT SCALLOP CEVICHE SKEWERS

MAKES 20

40 bay scallops or 20 sea scallops
grated peel and juice of 1 grapefruit
juice of 2 limes
4 tbsp olive oil
1 fresh red chili, seeded and finely chopped
½ red onion, finely chopped
½ tsp salt
1 tbsp finely chopped cilantro
1 scallion, finely sliced

ESSENTIAL EQUIPMENT
20 - 3in (7.5cm) wooden skewers or toothpicks

If using sea scallops, slice in half crosswise. Combine scallops, grapefruit, lime, oil, chili, onion, and salt in a non-metallic bowl. Cover and refrigerate for 3 hours, stirring occasionally. Remove scallops with a slotted spoon. Toss to coat with cilantro and scallion. Thread 2 bay scallops or 2 sea scallop halves onto each skewer. Serve chilled.

THINK AHEAD
Marinate scallops up to 6 hours in advance. Skewer scallops up to 3 hours in advance. Store in an airtight container in the refrigerator.

COOKS' NOTE
If you are uncomfortable about serving raw fish, you can use cooked, peeled medium shrimp instead of raw scallops in this recipe.

LEMON CHILI SHRIMP STICKS

MAKES 20

2 garlic cloves, crushed
½ in (1cm) piece fresh ginger, grated
2 tbsp finely chopped cilantro
½ tbsp chinese hot chili sauce
1 tbsp light soy sauce
1 tbsp honey
3 tbsp lemon juice
20 raw medium shrimp, peeled and deveined (see page 164)

ESSENTIAL EQUIPMENT
20 - 6in (15cm) wooden skewers presoaked in cold water

For marinade, combine garlic, ginger, cilantro, chili sauce, soy sauce, honey, and lemon in a non-metallic bowl. Add shrimp and toss in marinade to coat each one well. Cover and refrigerate for 1 hour. Thread 1 shrimp on to each presoaked skewer. Preheat broiler. Alternatively, preheat a ridged cast-iron griddle, broiler pan or barbecue. Broil shrimp until they turn pink and lose their transparency, 3 minutes on each side. Serve hot, warm or at room temperature.

THINK AHEAD
Marinate shrimp up to 4 hours in advance. Store in an airtight container in the refrigerator. Skewer shrimp up to 1 hour in advance. Store in an airtight container in the refrigerator.

SHRIMP AND SUGARCANE STICKS WITH MINTED CHILI DIPPING SAUCE

MAKES 20

4 - 4in (10cm) long sugarcane pieces
1lb (500g) raw shrimp, peeled and
deveined (see page 164)
2 garlic cloves, chopped
3 scallions, chopped
1 tbsp fish sauce
1 tsp sugar
1 tbsp cornstarch
1 egg white

1 tsp salt
½ tsp black pepper

FOR SAUCE
1 tbsp finely chopped mint
1 fresh green chili, seeded
and finely chopped
1 tbsp sugar
6 tbsp lime juice
6 tbsp fish sauce

Peel sugarcane with a vegetable peeler. Cut each sugarcane piece into ¼in (0.5cm) thick strips to make 20 sugarcane sticks (see page 148). Place shrimp, garlic, scallions, fish sauce, sugar, cornstarch, egg white, salt, and pepper in a food processor or blender; pulse to a smooth paste. Divide shrimp paste into 20 equal-sized pieces. With wet hands, place 1 piece of shrimp paste in the middle of your palm. Place sugarcane stick in the middle of the paste. Mold shrimp paste around the end of the stick. Repeat with remaining paste and sticks. Cover shrimp sticks and refrigerate for 30 minutes. For sauce, combine mint, chilli, sugar, lime, and fish sauce. Let stand at room temperature for 15 minutes to allow the flavors to blend.

Preheat broiler or barbecue. Broil shrimp sticks until golden and cooked through, 3 minutes on each side. Serve warm.

THINK AHEAD
Mold shrimp paste on to sugarcane sticks up to 4 hours in advance. Store in an airtight container in the refrigerator. Make dipping sauce without mint up to 3 days in advance. Cover and refrigerate. Add mint up to 3 hours before serving. Keep covered at room temperature.

COOKS' NOTE
You can find fresh, frozen or canned sugarcane from Asian food stores. Wooden skewers are less exotic but can be used for this fragrant shrimp paste.

SNOW PEA-WRAPPED SHRIMP SKEWERS WITH LEMON MAYONNAISE

MAKES 20

20 large snow peas
20 large shrimp, cooked and peeled
1 recipe lemon mayonnaise (see page 142)

ESSENTIAL EQUIPMENT
20 - 6in (15cm) wooden skewers

Bring a pan of water to a boil over hight heat. Add snow peas and boil for 1 minute. Drain and refresh them in cold water. Drain again and pat dry with paper towels.

Place 1 shrimp on top of each snow pea. Secure with skewer. Cover and refrigerate for 30 minutes. Serve chilled with lemon mayonnaise.

THINK AHEAD
Skewer shrimp and snow peas up to 8 hours in advance. Store in an airtight container in the refrigerator.

SALMON TERIYAKI SKEWERS WITH GINGER SOY DIPPING SAUCE

MAKES 20
¾ lb salmon fillet, 1in (2.5cm) thick

FOR GLAZE
3 tbsp sake
3 tbsp mirin
5 tbsp shoyu (japanese soy sauce)
1½ tbsp sugar

FOR SAUCE
½ in (1cm) piece fresh ginger, finely chopped
2 scallions, finely sliced
juice of 2 limes
6 tbsp shoyu (japanese soy sauce)

ESSENTIAL EQUIPMENT
20 - 6in (15cm) wooden skewers or chopsticks presoaked in cold water

Cut salmon into 20 - 1in (2.5cm) cubes.
For glaze, place sake, mirin, soy, and sugar in a small pan. Bring to a boil over medium heat. Simmer gently for 10 minutes until thick and syrupy. Cool.
For sauce, mix ginger, scallions, lime, and soy together. Let stand at room temperature for 15 minutes to allow the flavors to blend.
Toss salmon with cooled glaze in a non-metallic bowl to coat each piece well. Marinate at room temperature for 10 minutes. Thread 1 salmon cube on to 2 skewers or chopsticks.
Preheat broiler. Alternatively, preheat a ridged cast-iron griddle, broil pan or barbecue. Broil salmon skewers until firm to the touch, 2-3 minutes on each side. Serve hot or warm with ginger soy dipping sauce.

THINK AHEAD
Skewer salmon up to 3 hours in advance. Store in an airtight container in the refrigerator. Make dipping sauce without scallions up to 3 days in advance. Cover and refrigerate. Add scallions up to 3 hours before serving. Keep covered at room temperature.

MONKFISH, PANCETTA, AND ROSEMARY SPIEDINI WITH LEMON AIOLI

MAKES 20
¾ lb (350g) monkfish, boned and skinned
4 pancetta or bacon slices
20 - 4in (10cm) rosemary branches

FOR MARINADE
4 tbsp olive oil
grated peel and juice of ½ lemon
1 garlic clove, sliced
1 tsp salt, ½ tsp black pepper
1 recipe lemon aioli (see page 142)

Cut the monkfish into 20 - 1in (2.5cm) cubes. Cut pancetta or bacon into 20 equal-sized pieces. Cover the pieces and refrigerate.
For rosemary skewers, pull the leaves off the rosemary stalks, leaving just a few leaves at one end. Reserve leaves. Sharpen the other end into a point with a sharp paring knife (see page 148).
For marinade, roughly chop the reserved rosemary leaves. Combine rosemary, oil, lemon, garlic, salt, and pepper in a non-metallic bowl. Add monkfish and toss to coat each piece well. Cover and refrigerate for 30 minutes.
Thread 1 monkfish cube and 1 bacon piece onto the pointed end of each rosemary skewer. Preheat broiler. Alternatively, preheat a ridged cast-iron griddle, broiler pan or barbecue. Broil monkfish spiedini until cooked through, 2-3 minutes on each side. Serve warm with lemon aioli.

THINK AHEAD
Marinate monkfish up to 4 hours in advance. Store in an airtight container in the refrigerator. Skewer up to 2 hours in advance. Store in an airtight container in the refrigerator.

MOROCCAN SPICED SWORDFISH BROCHETTES

MAKES 20

¾ lb (350g) swordfish steak, 1in (2.5cm) thick

FOR MARINADE

1 red pepper, quartered and seeded

1 red chili, seeded and chopped

2 garlic cloves, chopped

2 tbsp chopped cilantro

2 tbsp chopped parsley

½ tsp ground coriander

1 tsp honey

grated peel and juice of ½ lemon

2 tbsp olive oil

1 tsp salt, ¼ tsp black pepper

ESSENTIAL EQUIPMENT

20 - 6in (15cm) wooden skewers presoaked in cold water

Cut swordfish into 20 - 1in (2.5cm) cubes. For marinade, broil and peel pepper quarters (see page 147). Place peeled pepper quarters, chili, garlic, fresh herbs, ground coriander, honey, lemon, oil, and salt and pepper in a food processor or blender; pulse to a thick paste. Toss swordfish and marinade together in a non-metallic bowl to coat each piece well. Cover and refrigerate for at least 30 minutes.

Thread 1 swordfish cube on to each presoaked skewer.

Preheat broiler. Alternatively, preheat a ridged cast-iron griddle, broiler pan or barbecue. Broil swordfish brochettes until cooked through, 2-3 minutes on each side. Serve hot or warm.

THINK AHEAD

Marinate swordfish up to 4 hours in advance. Store in an airtight container in the refrigerator. Skewer up to 2 hours in advance. Store in an airtight container in the refrigerator.

CHAR-BROILED MEDITERRANEAN TUNA SKEWERS WITH SPICY ROASTED TOMATO DIP

MAKES 20

¾ lb (350g) tuna steak, 1in (2.5cm) thick

FOR MARINADE

1 cup (15g) basil

1 cup (15g) parsley

2 garlic cloves

grated peel and juice of ½ lemon

2 tbsp olive oil

1 tsp salt

½ tsp black pepper

20 large basil leaves

FOR DIP

6 plum tomatoes, halved

1 red chili, seeded and chopped

2 garlic cloves, chopped

1 tbsp olive oil

1 tbsp balsamic vinegar

salt, black pepper

ESSENTIAL EQUIPMENT

20 - 6in (15cm) wooden skewers presoaked in cold water

For marinade, place basil, parsley, garlic, lemon, oil, salt, and pepper in a food processor or blender; pulse to a thick paste. Toss tuna and marinade together in a non-metallic bowl to coat each piece well. Cover and refrigerate for at least 30 minutes.

For dip, preheat oven to 400°F (200°C). Place tomatoes on an oven pan. Sprinkle over chili, garlic, oil, vinegar, and a pinch each salt and pepper. Roast until softened, 30 minutes. Place in a food processor or blender; pulse until smooth. Pass through a strainer to remove seeds. Add salt and pepper to taste. Keep warm.

Cut tuna into 1in (2.5cm) cubes. Wrap each tuna cube in a basil leaf. Thread 1 wrapped tuna cube on to each presoaked skewer. Preheat broiler. Alternatively, preheat a ridged cast-iron griddle, broiler pan or barbecue. Broil tuna skewers until cooked through, 2-3 minutes on each side. Serve hot or warm with spicy roast tomato dip.

THINK AHEAD

Make dip up to 2 days in advance. Cover and refrigerate. Marinate tuna up to 4 hours in advance. Store in an airtight container in the refrigerator. Skewer up to 2 hours in advance. Store in an airtight container in the refrigerator. Reheat dip just before serving.

COOKS' NOTE

Roasting tomatoes concentrates flavor and is a good treatment for out of season or less than ripe tomatoes.

LEMON AND SAFFRON CHICKEN BROCHETTES

MAKES 20

2 boneless, skinless chicken breast halves

FOR MARINADE

1 large pinch of saffron

½ medium onion, finely chopped

grated peel and juice of 1 lemon

4 tbsp olive oil

1 tsp salt, ½ tsp black pepper

ESSENTIAL EQUIPMENT

20 - 6in (15cm) wooden skewers presoaked in cold water

Cut chicken into 20 - 1in (2.5cm) cubes. For marinade, combine saffron, onion, lemon, oil, salt, and pepper in a non-metallic bowl. Add chicken and toss to coat each piece well. Cover and refrigerate for at least 1 hour. Thread 1 chicken cube on to each presoaked skewer. Preheat broiler. Alternatively, preheat a ridged cast-iron griddle, broiler pan or barbecue. Broilchicken brochettes until cooked through, 5 minutes on each side. Serve hot or warm.

THINK AHEAD
Marinate chicken up to 1 day in advance. Skewer chicken up to 12 hours in advance. Store in an airtight container in the refrigerator.

COOK'S NOTE
An important reminder: don't forget to presoak wooden skewers when using them in a broiling recipe. Allow the skewers to soak for at least 30 minutes in cold water to prevent them from scorching.

CURRIED COCONUT CHICKEN STICKS

MAKES 20

2 boneless, skinless chicken breast halves

FOR MARINADE

4 lemon grass stalks

1 tbsp curry powder

4 garlic cloves, chopped

2in (5cm) piece fresh ginger, chopped

2 shallots, chopped

½ cup (15g) cilantro

4 tbsp fish sauce

½ cup (125ml) canned coconut milk

1 tsp salt, ¼ tsp black pepper

ESSENTIAL EQUIPMENT

20 - 6in (15cm) wooden skewers presoaked in cold water

Cut chicken into 20 - 1in (2.5cm) cubes.
For marinade, remove and discard the tough outer skin from the lemon grass stalks and finely chop. Place lemon grass, curry powder, garlic, ginger, shallots, cilantro, fish sauce, coconut milk, salt, and pepper in a food processor or blender; pulse until smooth. Toss chicken and marinade together in a non-metallic bowl to coat each piece well. Cover and refrigerate for at least 1 hour.
Thread 1 chicken cube on to each presoaked skewer. Preheat broiler. Alternatively, preheat a ridged cast-iron griddle, broiler pan or barbecue. Broil chicken sticks until cooked through, 5 minutes on each side. Serve hot, warm or at room temperature.

THINK AHEAD
Marinate chicken up to 1 day in advance. Skewer chicken up to 12 hours in advance. Store in an airtight container in the refrigerator.

THAI CHICKEN AND LEMON GRASS STICKS WITH SWEET CUCUMBER DIPPING SAUCE

MAKES 20

11 lemon grass stalks

2 boneless, skinless chicken breasts

2 garlic cloves, chopped

1 red chilli, seeded and chopped

2 tbsp chopped cilantro

1 tsp brown sugar

1 tsp salt

FOR SAUCE

½ cup (125ml) rice vinegar

½ cup (125ml) sugar

2 garlic cloves, finely chopped

2 red chilies, seeded and finely chopped

½ tsp salt

¼ cucumber, seeded and finely diced

1 tbsp finely chopped cilantro

For lemon grass sticks, remove and discard the tough outer skin from the lemongrass. Set 1 stalk aside to flavor the chicken. Cut each of the 10 remaining lemon grass stalks in half lengthwise, keeping the stalks attached by the root. Trim to 5in (12.5cm) lengths (see page 148). Place the reserved lemon grass stalk, chicken, garlic, chili, cilantro, sugar, and salt in a food processor; pulse until smooth. Divide into 20 equal-sized pieces. With wet hands, roll into oval shapes. Skewer each chicken oval onto the pointed end of a lemon grass length. Cover and refrigerate for 30 minutes to allow the flavors to blend. For sauce, bring vinegar and sugar to a boil in a pan over medium heat. Simmer gently until syrupy, 5 minutes. Pour syrup over garlic, chilies, and salt in a separate bowl; cool. Stir in cucumber and cilantro when cool. Let stand for 15 minutes at room temperature to allow the flavors to blend. Preheat broiler. Alternatively, preheat a ridged cast-iron griddle, broiler pan, or barbecue. Broil chicken lemon grass sticks until cooked through, 5 minutes on each side. Serve hot or at room temperature with the dipping sauce.

THINK AHEAD

Prepare and skewer chicken up to 12 hours in advance. Store in an airtight container in the refrigerator. Make sauce without cucumber and cilantro up to 3 days in advance. Cover and refrigerate. Add cucumber and cilantro up to 3 hours before serving. Keep covered at room temperature.

CHICKEN, PROSCIUTTO, AND SAGE SPIEDINI WITH ROAST PEPPER AIOLI

MAKES 20

FOR AIOLI

1 red pepper, quartered and seeded

1 recipe lemon aioli (see page 142)

FOR SPIEDINI

2 boneless, skinless chicken breast halves

2 tbsp lemon juice

1 garlic clove, crushed

1 tsp salt

½ tsp black pepper

4 tbsp olive oil

5 prosciutto slices

20 sage leaves

4 slices day-old baguette, 1in (2.5cm) thick

ESSENTIAL EQUIPMENT

20 -6in (15cm) wooden skewers presoaked in cold water

For aioli, broil and peel pepper quarters (see page 147). Place peeled pepper quarters in a food processor or blender; pulse to a smooth purée. Stir pepper purée into aioli. Let stand at room temperature for 15 minutes to allow the flavors to combine.

For spiedini, cut chicken into 1in (2.5cm) cubes. Toss chicken together with lemon, garlic, salt, pepper, and 4 tbsp oil in a non-metallic bowl to coat each piece well. Cut each prosciutto slice into 4 strips. Place 1 sage leaf on each prosciutto strip. Top with 1 chicken cube. Wrap sage and prosciutto around chicken. Repeat with remaining chicken.

Cut baguette slices into 20 - 1in (2.5cm) cubes. Thread 1 bread cube and 1 prosciutto-wrapped chicken cube on to each presoaked skewer. Brush bread with remaining oil.

Preheat broiler. Alternatively, preheat a ridged cast-iron griddle, broiler pan or barbecue. Broil chicken spiedini until cooked through, 5 minutes on each side. Serve warm or at room temperature with roast pepper aioli.

THINK AHEAD

Make aioli up to 3 days in advance. Cover and refrigerate. Skewer chicken up to 12 hours in advance. Store in an airtight container in the refrigerator.

CHICKEN YAKITORI

MAKES 20

¾ lb (350g) boneless, skinless chicken
thighs

FOR MARINADE

4 tbsp shoyu (japanese soy sauce)

2 tbsp mirin

1½ tbsp sake

1 tsp sugar

5 shiitake mushrooms

2 scallions

ESSENTIAL EQUIPMENT

*20 - 6in (15cm) wooden skewers presoaked in
cold water*

Cut chicken into 20 - 1in (2.5cm) pieces.
For marinade, place soy, mirin, sake,
and sugar in a small pan. Bring to a boil
over a medium heat. Simmer gently until
slightly syrupy, 5 minutes. Cool.
Toss marinade and chicken together in a
non-metallic bowl to coat each piece
well. Cover and refrigerate for at least
30 minutes.
Cut mushrooms into quarters. Cut
scallions in 20 - 1in (2.5cm) lengths.
Thread 1 scallion piece, 1 chicken cube,
and 1 mushroom quarter on to each
presoaked skewer. Preheat broiler.
Alternatively, preheat a ridged cast-iron
griddle, broiler pan, or barbecue. Broil
chicken yakitori until cooked through,
5 minutes on each side. Serve hot.

THINK AHEAD
Marinate chicken up to 3 hours in advance. Assemble
skewers up to 1 hour in advance. Store in an airtight
container in the refrigerator.

LIME MARINATED CHICKEN SKEWERS WITH AVOCADO CREMA DIP

MAKES 20

2 boneless, skinless chicken breast halves

FOR MARINADE

juice of 1 lime

1 tbsp honey

2 tbsp olive oil

2 green chilies, seeded and finely chopped

½ cup (15g) cilantro, finely chopped

1tsp salt, ¼ tsp black pepper

ESSENTIAL EQUIPMENT

*20 - 6in (15cm) wooden skewers presoaked in
cold water*

FOR DIP

1 avocado, stoned

3 scallions, chopped

1 tbsp red wine vinegar

1 tbsp olive oil

½ cup (125ml) sour cream

salt, black pepper

1 tbsp finely chopped cilantro to
garnish

Cut chicken into 1in (2.5cm) cubes.
For marinade, combine lime, honey, oil, chilies, cilantro, salt, and pepper in a
non-metallic bowl. Add chicken and toss to coat each piece well. Cover and
refrigerate for at least 1 hour.
For dip, place avocado, scallions, vinegar, olive oil, and sour cream in a food
processor or blender; pulse until smooth. Add salt and pepper to taste. Cover and
refrigerate for 30 minutes to allow the flavors to blend.
Thread a chicken cube on to each presoaked skewer. Preheat broiler. Alternatively,
preheat a ridged cast-iron griddle, broiler pan or barbecue. Broil chicken skewers
until cooked through, 5 minutes on each side. Garnish each skewer with a
sprinkling of cilantro. Serve warm with avocado crema dip.

THINK AHEAD
Marinate chicken up to 1 day in advance. Skewer chicken up to 12 hours in advance. Store in an airtight container in the refrigerator. Make dip up to 8 hours in advance. Cover and refrigerate.

COOKS' NOTE
To prevent the avocado crema dip from discoloring when making ahead, make sure you press a piece of plastic wrap directly on to the surface of the dip. It's the oxygen in the air that turns avocado brown, so the less air
that comes into contact with the dip, the better.

SPICY SATAY STICKS

MAKES 20

2 boneless, skinless chicken breast halves

FOR MARINADE
1 lemon grass stalk
2 shallots
2 garlic cloves
½ in (1cm) piece fresh ginger
2 tsp brown sugar
½ tsp ground cumin
½ tsp ground cilantro
1 tsp turmeric
1 tsp salt
1 tbsp sunflower oil

ESSENTIAL EQUIPMENT
20 - 6in (15cm) wooden skewers presoaked in cold water

FOR SAUCE
4 tbsp roasted peanuts
2 lemon grass stalks
2 shallots
2 garlic cloves
1in (2.5cm) piece fresh ginger
1 tsp turmeric
1 tbsp sunflower oil
1 tbsp brown sugar
1 tsp fish sauce
1 tbsp chinese hot chili sauce
juice of 1 lime
4 tbsp water
½ cup (125ml) canned coconut milk

Slice chicken into 20 strips about ¼ in (0.5cm) thick and 2½ in (6cm) long.

For marinade, remove and discard the tough outer skin from the lemon grass and finely chop. Place lemon grass, shallots, garlic, ginger, sugar, spices, salt, and oil in a food processor or blender; pulse to a smooth paste. Toss chicken and marinate together in a non-metallic bowl to coat each piece well. Cover and refrigerate for at least 1 hour.

For sauce, place peanuts in a food processor or blender; pulse until finely ground. Set aside. Remove and discard the tough outer skin from the lemon grass and finely chop. Place shallots, garlic, ginger, chopped lemon grass, turmeric, and sunflower oil in a food processor or blender; pulse to a smooth paste. Heat a frying pan over a medium heat. Add paste and stir fry until softened, 5 minutes. Stir in ground peanuts, sugar, fish sauce, and chili sauce, lime, water, and coconut milk. Cook, stirring occasionally, until the sauce thickens, 10 minutes. Keep warm.

Thread 1 chicken strip on to each presoaked skewer, running the skewer through it like a ruffled ribbon. Preheat broiler. Alternatively, preheat a ridged cast-iron griddle, broiler pan or barbecue. Broil chicken satay sticks until cooked through, 5 minutes on each side. Serve hot with warm satay sauce.

THINK AHEAD
Make sauce up 4 days in advance. Cover and refrigerate. Marinate chicken up to 1 day in advance. Skewer chicken up to 12 hours in advance. Store in an airtight container in the refrigerator. Reheat sauce before serving.

COOKS' NOTE
The satay sauce will thicken on standing, so, if making ahead, bear in mind that you may need to thin it down with a tablespoon or so of lime juice when you reheat.

CUMIN SCENTED KOFTE BROCHETTES WITH MINTED YOGURT DIP

MAKES 20

¾ lb (350g) lean minced lamb

1 medium onion, grated

2 garlic cloves, chopped

2 tsp ground cumin

½ tsp ground coriander

grated peel of 1 lemon

2 tbsp finely chopped cilantro

1½ tsp salt

¼ tsp cayenne pepper

FOR DIP

¾ cup (175ml) whole-milk yogurt

½ cup (15g) mint, finely chopped

½ cup (15g) parsley, finely chopped

juice of ½ lemon

salt, cayenne pepper

ESSENTIAL EQUIPMENT

20 - 6in (15cm) wooden skewers presoaked in cold water

Place lamb, onion, garlic, cumin, ground coriander, lemon, fresh cilantro, salt, and cayenne pepper in a food processor; pulse until combined and slightly pasty. Divide into 20 equal-sized pieces. With wet hands, roll into oval shapes. Thread 1 oval on to each presoaked skewer. Cover and refrigerate for 30 minutes. For dip, combine yogurt, mint, parsley, and lemon. Add salt and cayenne pepper to taste. Cover and refrigerate for 30 minutes to allow the flavors to blend. Preheat broiler. Alternatively, preheat a ridged cast-iron griddle, broiler pan or barbecue. Broil brochettes until browned but still pink and juicy inside, 3 minutes on each side. Serve hot with chilled minted yogurt dip.

THINK AHEAD

Make dip up to 1 day in advance. Cover and refrigerate. Prepare and skewer kofte up to 12 hours in advance. Store in an airtight container in the refrigerator.

SESAME SOY GLAZED BEEF SKEWERS

MAKES 20

¾ lb (350g) beef fillet or sirloin, 1in (2.5cm) thick

4 scallions, white stalk only

1 red pepper, halved and seeded

FOR GLAZE

2 tbsp sesame seeds

2 lemon grass stalks, tender stalk only, finely chopped

1 tbsp honey

2 tbsp sesame oil

1 tbsp sunflower oil

2 tbsp light soy sauce

1 tbsp chinese hot chili sauce

½ tsp black pepper

1 tsp salt

ESSENTIAL EQUIPMENT

20 - 6in (15cm) wooden skewers presoaked in cold water

Cut beef into 20 - 1in (2.5cm) cubes. Cut scallions diagonally into 20 - 1in (2.5cm) lengths. Cut pepper into 20 - 1in (2.5cm) pieces.

For glaze, combine seeds, lemon grass, honey, oils, soy sauce, chili sauce, black pepper, and salt in a non-metallic bowl. Add beef, scallions, and peppers. Toss to coat each piece well. Cover and refrigerate for at least 1 hour.

Thread 1 piece each of scallion and pepper and 1 beef cube on to each presoaked skewer.

Preheat broiler. Alternatively, preheat ridged cast-iron griddle, broiler pan or barbecue. Broil beef skewers until browned but still pink and juicy inside, 3 minutes on each side. Serve hot.

THINK AHEAD

Marinate beef up to 1 day in advance. Store in an airtight container in the refrigerator. Skewer beef up to 12 hours in advance. Store in an airtight container in the refrigerator.

MINT MARINATED LAMB KEBABS WITH TAHINI AND HONEY DIP

MAKES 20

¾lb (350g) lean boneless lamb

FOR MARINADE

½ cup (30g) mint, finely chopped
2 garlic cloves, crushed
1 tbsp honey
2 tbsp lemon juice
2 tbsp olive oil
1 tsp salt
½ tsp pepper

FOR DIP

2 tbsp sesame seeds
2 tsp honey
juice of 1 lemon
5 tbsp tahini
½ cup (125ml) whole-milk yogurt
3 tbsp water
salt, black pepper

ESSENTIAL EQUIPMENT
20 - 6in (15cm) wooden skewers presoaked in cold water

Cut lamb into 20 - 1in (2.5cm) cubes.
For marinade, combine half of the chopped mint, garlic, honey, lemon juice, oil, salt, and pepper. Add lamb and toss to coat each piece well. Cover and refrigerate. Marinate for at least 1 hour.
For dip, toast seeds in a dry pan over low heat until nutty and golden, 3 minutes. Combine seeds, honey, lemon, tahini, yogurt and water. Add salt and pepper to taste. Cover and refrigerate. Leave for 30 minutes for the flavors to blend.
Thread 1 lamb cube on to each presoaked skewer. Preheat broiler. Alternatively, preheat ridged cast-iron griddle, broiler pan or barbecue. Broil lamb kebabs until browned but still pink and juicy inside, 3 minutes on each side. Garnish each kebab with a sprinkling of the remaining mint. Serve hot with chilled tahini and honey dip.

THINK AHEAD
Make dip up to 2 days in advance. Cover and refrigerate. Marinate lamb up to 1 day in advance. Skewer lamb up to 12 hours in advance. Store in an airtight container in the refrigerator.

GINGER ORANGE PORK SKEWERS

MAKES 20

¾lb (350g) lean boneless pork

FOR MARINADE

2in (5cm) piece fresh ginger, peeled and grated
grated peel of 1 orange
juice of ½ orange
2 tsp creamy dijon mustard
2 tsp honey

1 tbsp balsamic vinegar
2 tbsp light soy sauce
4 tbsp olive oil
1 tsp salt
½ tsp black pepper
2in (5cm) piece fresh ginger for garnish

ESSENTIAL EQUIPMENT
20 - 6in (15cm) wooden skewers presoaked in cold water

Cut pork into 20 -1in (2.5cm) cubes. Combine grated ginger, orange, mustard, honey, vinegar, soy, oil, salt, and pepper in a non-metallic bowl. Add pork and toss to coat each piece well. Cover and refrigerate for at least 1 hour.
For garnish, preheat oven to 400°F (200°C). Cut ginger piece for garnish into fine slices. Cut ginger slices into julienne (see page 147). Bring a pan of water to a boil over high heat. Add ginger julienne and boil for 1 minute. Drain. Spread ginger julienne in a single layer on a baking sheet. Bake until crispy and dry, 5-10 minutes. Cool.
Preheat broiler. Alternatively, preheat ridged cast-iron griddle, broiler pan or barbecue. Broil pork skewers until cooked through, 5 minutes on each side. Sprinkle each skewer with crisp ginger garnish. Serve hot.

THINK AHEAD
Make crisp ginger garnish up to 2 days in advance. Store in an airtight container at room temperature. Marinate pork up to 1 day in advance. Store in an airtight container in the refrigerator. Skewer pork up to 12 hours in advance. Store in an airtight container in the refrigerator.

TROPICAL FRUIT BROCHETTES WITH PASSION FRUIT AND MASCARPONE DIP

MAKES 20

1 firm mango

2 firm kiwi

¼ watermelon

FOR DIP

2 passion fruit, halved

¼ cup (200g) mascarpone cheese

1 tbsp honey

1 tbsp grated orange peel

ESSENTIAL EQUIPMENT

20 wooden toothpicks

Cut each fruit into 20 - ¾in (2cm) cubes. Thread 3 different fruit cubes on to each skewer. Cover and refrigerate for 30 minutes.

For dip, spoon passion fruit pulp out from the center of each half with a teaspoon. Sieve pulp and discard seeds. Combine passion fruit pulp, mascarpone, honey, and orange. Cover and refrigerate for 30 minutes. Serve chilled tropical fruit brochettes with chilled passion fruit and mascarpone dip.

THINK AHEAD

Make dip up to 1 day in advance. Cover and refrigerate. Skewer fruit up to 4 hours in advance. Cover and refrigerate.

COOKS' NOTE

These brochettes are open to variation. Use your favorite combination of tropical fruit. For the prettiest brochettes, think about complimentary colors as well as flavors. Try to select firm, just ripe fruits that will cube and skewer easily.

PROSCIUTTO-WRAPPED FIG SKEWERS

MAKES 20

10 very thin prosciutto slices

3½oz (100g) parmesan cheese

5 ripe figs, quartered

black pepper

½ tbsp grated parmesan cheese

ESSENTIAL EQUIPMENT

vegetable peeler

20 - 6in (15cm) wooden skewers

Cut each prosciutto slice lengthwise into 2 strips. Shave the parmesan with a vegetable peeler to make 20 shavings (see page 148). Place 1 parmesan shaving on each prosciutto strip. Place 1 fig quarter on top. Sprinkle with a pinch of pepper. Wrap up the fig in prosciutto. Secure with skewer. Sprinkle with grated parmesan just before serving. Serve chilled or at room temperature.

THINK AHEAD

Skewer figs up to 4 hours in advance. Cover and refrigerate.

COOKS' NOTE

Firm melon and papaya slices make suitable substitutes when figs are not in season. Speck, coppa, or serrano are a few of the huge wealth of cured hams that are suitable alternatives to prosciutto. To make wrapping easy, make sure any ham you choose is sliced very thin.

CHERUBS ON HORSEBACK

MAKES 20

20 ready soaked dried apricots

10 slices of bacon

ESSENTIAL EQUIPMENT

20 wooden toothpicks presoaked in cold water

Preheat oven 400°F (200°C).

Cut the bacon in half crosswise. Stretch each piece of bacon by running the back of a knife along the bacon slice. This will help prevent shrinking during cooking. Wrap 1 bacon piece around each apricot. Secure with a presoaked skewer. Place skewered apricots on a baking pan. Bake until bacon is crisp, 10 minutes. Serve hot or warm.

THINK AHEAD

Skewer apricots up to 1 day in advance. Store in an airtight container in the refrigerator.

BASIL MARINATED MOZZARELLA AND CHERRY TOMATO SKEWERS

MAKES 20

1 red pepper, quartered and seeded
1 garlic clove, finely chopped
1 tbsp lemon juice
2 tbsp olive oil
½ tsp salt
1 tsp cracked black pepper
¾ lb (approximately 20 pieces) bocconcini,
(see cook's note)
1 cup (15g) basil, finely chopped
20 cherry tomatoes, halved
20 large basil leaves

ESSENTIAL EQUIPMENT
20 - 15cm (6in) wooden skewers

LEMON MARINATED TORTELLINI AND SUN-DRIED TOMATO SKEWERS

MAKES 20

½ lb (approximately 20 pieces) fresh
spinach and ricotta tortellini
10 sun-dried tomatoes in oil,
drained and halved
20 large basil leaves

FOR MARINADE

1 tsp grated lemon peel
2 tbsp lemon juice
4 tbsp olive oil
salt, black pepper

ESSENTIAL EQUIPMENT
20 - 6in (15cm) wooden skewers

Cook tortellini in salted boiling water
until tender, 4 minutes, or according to
instructions on the package. Drain and
rinse with cold water. Spread out in a
single layer on a clean dish towel to dry.
For marinade, whisk lemon and oil until
thick and combined. Toss the cooled
pasta and marinade together in a
non-metallic bowl to coat each piece
well. Add salt and pepper to taste.
Cover and marinate at room
temperature for 30 minutes.
Thread 1 tortellini and 1 sun-dried
tomato half wrapped in 1 basil leaf on to
each skewer. Serve at room
temperature.

THINK AHEAD
Marinate tortellini up to 1 day in advance. Cover and
refrigerate. Assemble skewers up to 4 hours in
advance. Return to room temperature before serving.

Broil and peel pepper quarters (see page
147). Cut pepper quarters into very fine
dice (see page 147). Combine pepper
dice, garlic, lemon, oil, salt, and cracked
pepper in a non-metallic bowl. Add
bocconcini and toss to coat each piece
well. Cover and marinate at room
temperature for at least 30 minutes.
Sprinkle basil over and toss to coat each
bocconcini well. Thread 1 cherry tomato
half and 1 bocconcini onto each skewer.
Wrap each remaining cherry tomato half
in 1 basil leaf and add 1 to each skewer.
Serve chilled or at room temperature.

THINK AHEAD
Marinate bocconcini up to 3 days in advance. Store in
an airtight container in the refrigerator. Assemble
skewers up to 4 hours in advance. Cover and
refrigerate.

COOKS' NOTE
Bocconcini means "mouthful" in Italian. If you can't
find baby mozzarella balls, about ¾ in diameter, cut
larger ones into ¾ in (2cm) cubes; then marinate
and skewer as directed.

FENNEL MARINATED FETA AND OLIVE SKEWERS

MAKES 20

2 tbsp sesame seeds
7oz (200g) feta cheese
1 tbsp fennel seeds
grated peel of 1 lemon
1 tbsp lemon juice
2 tbsp olive oil
1½ tsp cracked black pepper
¾ cup (15g) mint, finely chopped
20 mint leaves
½ cucumber, peeled and seeded
10 pitted black olives, halved

ESSENTIAL EQUIPMENT
20 - 6in (5cm) wooden skewers

Toast seeds in a dry pan over low heat
until nutty and golden, 3 minutes. Cool.
Gently rinse feta in cold water. Drain on
kitchen paper. Cut feta into ¾in (2cm)
cubes. Toss feta together with fennel,
toasted sesame seeds, lemon, oil, and
pepper to coat each cube well. Cover
and refrigerate for 4 hours to allow the
flavors to combine.
Sprinkle feta with chopped mint and
toss to coat each cube well. Cut
cucumber into 20- ½in (1cm) cubes.
Thread 1 mint leaf, 1 olive half, 1
cucumber cube, and 1 feta cube on to
each skewer. Serve chilled or at room
temperature.

THINK AHEAD
Marinate feta up to 3 days in advance. Store in an
airtight container in the refrigerator. Skewer feta up
to 4 hours in advance. Cover and refrigerate.

WRAPS AND ROLLS

SPINACH, SMOKED TROUT AND HERBED CREAM ROULADE

MAKES 30

FOR ROULADE

12 cups (350g) spinach

3 eggs, separated

1 tsp salt

½ tsp black pepper

¼ tsp ground nutmeg

FOR FILLING

8oz pkg (200g) cream cheese

2 tbsp finely chopped fresh dill

grated peel and juice of 1 lemon

salt, black pepper

½lb (200g) smoked salmon slices

ESSENTIAL EQUIPMENT

14 x 10in (35 x 25cm) jelly roll pan lined with buttered baking parchment

Preheat oven to 400°F (200°F).

Bring a pan of water to a boil and add spinach. When the water returns to a boil, drain and refresh the spinach in cold water. Squeeze spinach dry with hands. Place spinach, egg yolks, salt, pepper, and nutmeg in a food processor or blender; pulse to a smooth purée. Beat egg whites until they hold soft peaks (see page 141). Fold egg whites lightly into the spinach until evenly combined. Spread spinach mixture into the prepared tray. Bake until set, 10-12 minutes. Turn baked roulade out on to a sheet of baking parchment. Let it cool.

For filling, combine cream cheese, dill, lemon peel, and juice. Add salt and pepper to taste. Peel off tray lining paper. Cut roulade in half crosswize. Place each half on a piece of plastic wrap. Spread filling evenly over both roulade halves, to within about ½ in (1cm) of the edges. Cover each with a layer of salmon slices. Sprinkle with black pepper. Roll up each roulade half from the long edge (see page 148). Wrap in plastic wrap, twisting the ends to secure (see page 148). Refrigerate rolls 1hour. With a serrated knife, trim ends of both roulades. Cut each roulade into 10 slices. Discard plastic wrap after slicing. Serve chilled or at room temperature.

THINK AHEAD

Make roulade up to 1 day in advance. Refrigerate. Slice up to 1 hour before serving.

ROLLED PARSLEY FRITTATINE WITH BLACK OLIVE RICOTTA

MAKES 20

FOR FRITTATINE

3 eggs, beaten

3 tbsp heavy cream

1 tbsp melted butter

1 tbsp finely chopped parsley

⅛ tsp ground nutmeg

½ tsp salt, ¼ tsp pepper

1 tsp butter for pan

FOR FILLING

½ cup (125g) ricotta cheese

1 cup (150g) pitted black olives, finely chopped

salt, black pepper

ESSENTIAL EQUIPMENT

9in (24cm) non-stick or heavy frying pan

Beat eggs, cream, melted butter, parsley, nutmeg, salt, and pepper until combined. Melt half of the butter in pan over medium heat. Pour in half of egg mixture. Cook until golden and set on both sides, 5 minutes in total. Slide frittatine from pan on to kitchen paper to drain. Repeat with remaining butter and egg mixture. Let it cool. For filling, combine ricotta and olives. Add salt and pepper to taste. Spread each cooled frittatina evenly with half of the filling to within ½in (1cm) of edges. Roll up separately. Wrap each in plastic wrap, twisting the ends to secure (see page 148). Refrigerate 1 hour. With a serrated knife, trim ends of both frittatina. Cut each frittatina into 10 slices. Discard the plastic wrap after slicing. Serve chilled or at room temperature.

THINK AHEAD

Make frittatine up to 1 day in advance. Refrigerate. Slice up to 1 hour before serving.

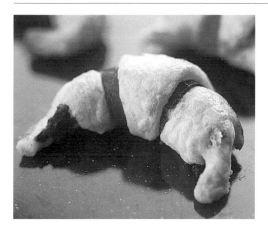

HAM AND DIJON MINI CROISSANTS

MAKES 20
8oz pkg (250g) puff pastry
3 tbsp creamy dijon mustard
4oz (125g) ham slices
1 egg yolk beaten with 1 tbsp water

Preheat oven to 400°F (200°C).
Roll out pastry to 18in x 7in (45cm x 18cm) rectangle. Trim uneven edges with a sharp knife. Cut pastry in half lengthwise to make 2 strips each 3½in (9cm) wide. Cut each strip diagonally into 10 even-sized triangles (see below, left). Cut ham into strips about 4in (10cm) long and ¼in (0.5cm) wide.

Spread each pastry triangle with mustard. Place ham on longest edge. Roll up each triangle, starting at the long edge and ending with the point (see below, right). Place on a greased baking sheet. Curl ends in to make a crescent. Tuck the points underneath to prevent the croissants from unravelling as they bake. Brush croissants with beaten egg. Bake until crisp and golden, 10 minutes. Cool on wire rack. Serve warm or at room temperature.

THINK AHEAD
Bake up to 3 days in advance. Store in an airtight container at room temperature. Crisp in preheated 400°F (200°C) oven, 3 minutes.

SMOKED SALMON RUGGELASH

MAKES 32
FOR PASTRY
4 oz pkg (90g) cream cheese
6 tbsp (90g) cold butter, diced
1 cup (125g) all-purpose flour
pinch salt
FOR FILLING
1/2lb (200g) smoked salmon slices
1 tbsp lemon juice
¼ tsp black pepper
1 tbsp finely chopped fresh dill
1 egg yolk beaten with 1 tbsp water

Preheat oven to 400°F (200°C) .
Place cream cheese, butter, flour, and salt in a food processor; pulse until smooth dough forms. Refrigerate 30 minutes. Divide pastry into 2 equal-sized pieces. Roll out each piece to a 9in (23cm) round. Cover each round with a single layer of smoked salmon slices. Cut each round across into 16 even-sized triangles. Sprinkle with lemon, pepper, and dill. Roll up each triangle, starting at the long edge and ending with the point. Place on a greased baking sheet. Curl ends in to make a crescent. Tuck the points underneath to prevent the ruggelash from unravelling as they bake. Refrigerate until firm, 20 minutes. Brush ruggelash with beaten egg. Bake until crisp and golden, 10 minutes. Cool on wire rack. Serve warm.

THINK AHEAD
Bake up to 3 days in advance. Store in an airtight container at room temperature. Crisp in preheated 400°F (200°C) oven, 3 minutes.

OLIVE CHEESE BALLS

MAKES 20
20 pitted large green olives
1 cup (75g) parmesan cheese, grated
4 tbsp (60g) cold butter, diced
¾ cup (100g) all- purpose flour
salt, cayenne pepper
1 egg yolk beaten with 1 tbsp water
1 tsp poppy seeds

Preheat oven 350°F (180°C).
Pat olives dry with kitchen paper. Place parmesan, butter, and flour with pinch each salt and cayenne pepper in a food processor; pulse until smooth pastry forms. Divide pastry into 20 equal-sized pieces. With floured hands, press 1 piece of pastry around each olive to enclose completely. Roll pastry-wrapped olives between palms of your hands to make smooth, olive shapes. Place on a greased baking sheet. Refrigerate until firm, 30 minutes. Brush pastry with beaten egg. Sprinkle with seeds. Bake until golden, 20 minutes. Cool on a wire rack. Serve warm or at room temperature.

THINK AHEAD
Bake up to 3 days in advance. Store in an airtight container at room temperature. Crisp in preheated 400°F (200°C) oven, 3 minutes.

COOKS' NOTE
If you can't find pitted large green olives, use 30 regular pitted olives instead.

Mark out the triangle shapes with the back of a knife before cutting.

SPICY PORK EMPANADITAS WITH CHUNKY AVOCADO RELISH

MAKES 20

FOR FILLING
1 tbsp sunflower oil
½ medium onion, finely chopped
⅓lb (175g) ground pork
3 garlic cloves, finely chopped
1 red chili, seeded and
finely chopped
½ tsp ground cumin
¼ tsp ground cinnamon
pinch of ground cloves
½ cup (125ml) tomato juice
1 tsp tomato purée
2 tbsp raisins
10 pimento-stuffed green olives,
chopped
salt, black pepper

FOR PASTRY
1½ cups(175g) flour
½ tsp salt
2tbsp (30g) butter
⅓ cup(90ml) warm water

ESSENTIAL EQUIPMENT
1 - 2¾ in (6.5) plain pastry cutter

FOR RELISH
½ medium onion, finely
chopped
2 red chilies, seeded and
finely chopped
2 tomatoes, peeled, seeded
and finely chopped
(see page 147)
1 garlic clove, finely
chopped
2 tbsp finely chopped
cilantro
juice of 1 lime
2 medium avocados
salt

For filling, heat oil in a frying pan over medium heat. Stir fry onions in oil until soft, 5 minutes. Add pork. Stir pork constantly with a fork to break up any lumps until lightly browned, 5 minutes. Add garlic and chilies; cook until fragrant, 3 minutes. Add spices, tomato juice, tomato purée, raisins, and olives. Reduce heat to low and simmer, stirring occasionally, until thick, 15 minutes. Cool. Add salt and pepper to taste. Cover and refrigerate until chilled, 30 minutes.

For pastry, sift flour and salt into a bowl. Rub butter into the flour with fingers until mixture resembles fine crumbs. Use a fork to stir in the water to make a firm dough. Turn dough on to a lightly floured surface and knead until smooth, 3 minutes. Wrap dough in plastic wrap and let rest at room temperature for 30 minutes. Roll out dough to a ⅛ in (2mm) thickness. Cut out 20 rounds with the pastry cutter. Place 1 tsp of filling in center of each round. Fold pastry over filling to make crescents. Pinch edges firmly together to seal. With fingertips, seal edges (see opposite).

Place empanaditas on greased baking sheets. Brush with beaten egg. Bake until crisp and golden, 15 minutes. Cool on a wire rack.

For relish, combine onion, chili, tomato, garlic, cilantro and lime. Cut avocados into 1in (2.5cm) cubes. Mash the avocado into the onion mixture while combining with the other ingredients. Add salt to taste. Cover plastic wrap tightly over the surface of the relish. Refrigerate for 15 minutes. Serve empanaditas warm or at room temperature with relish for dipping.

EMPANADITAS FILLING VARIATIONS

SPICY CHORIZO EMPANADITAS

Use ⅓lb (175g) skinned and crumbled chorizo sausage instead of minced pork when making the filling.

HOT PEPPER AND SMOKY MOZZARELLA EMPANADITAS

Make hot pepper relish (see page 119). Fill empanaditas with 1 tsp grated smoked mozzarella and 1 tsp relish instead of spicy pork.

THINK AHEAD
Assemble empanaditas up to 1 day in advance. Cover and refrigerate. Bake empanaditas up to 8 hours in advance. Keep at room temperature. Make relish up to 3 hours in advance. Cover tightly with plastic wrap and refrigerate.

COOKS' NOTE
The secret to juicy empanaditas is to chill the filling before assembling. The juices in the filling will solidify so that the empanaditas won't leak as they are assembled. Press a piece of plastic wrap directly on to the surface of the relish to keep out the air that causes the avocado to darken. If the relish does discolor slightly, simply scrape off the dark surface. The relish will still be green underneath.

CRAB AND PAPAYA RICE PAPER ROLLS WITH SWEET CHILI DIPPING SAUCE

MAKES 20

¼lb (125g) white crab meat
2 scallions, cut into julienne strips (see page 147)
½ cucumber, seeded and cut into julienne strips (see page 147)
10 sheets of rice paper
1 papaya, quartered and finely sliced
20 mint leaves
20 basil leaves

FOR SAUCE

2 tbsp sugar
2 tbsp boiling water
2 tbsp fish sauce
2 tbsp lime juice
1 tbsp rice vinegar
1 red chili, seeded and chopped
1 garlic, crushed

Divide the crab, scallions, and cucumber strips into 20 equal-sized portions.
Pour about ¾in (1.5cm) cold water into a shallow dish. Dip 1 sheet of rice paper into the water and leave until softened, 2 minutes. Remove and spread out on a dry dish towel. Cut in half. Top 1 half with 1 portion of crab, scallion and cucumber. Place 1 papaya slice, 1 mint leaf, and 1 basil leaf on top of the cucumber so that they stick out slightly over the straight end of the rice paper. Roll rice paper over to enclose filling. Fold one end of the rice paper over the enclosed filling to make a 2in (5cm) cylinder. Continue rolling up into a cylinder and press the end with a wet finger to seal. Place the roll, seal side down on a tray and cover with a dampened dish towel to keep moist. Repeat with the remaining half sheet rice paper, then start again with remaining rice paper sheets and filling.
For sauce, dissolve sugar in boiling water. Combine dissolved sugar, fish sauce, lime, vinegar, chili and garlic.
Serve rice paper rolls chilled or at room temperature with sweet chili dipping sauce.

THINK AHEAD
Prepare filling ingredients up to 1 day in advance. Cover and refrigerate. Make rolls up to 3 hours in advance. Cover with a dampened dish towel and refrigerate. Be sure to keep the dish towel moist.

COOKS' NOTE
Rice paper is fragile and fiddly to work with. Be prepared to discard some rice papers if they tear and have extra rice papers in reserve to replace them.

Enclose prawn in rice paper.

FRESH HERB AND SHRIMP RICE PAPER ROLLS WITH PEANUT HOISIN DIPPING SAUCE

MAKES 20

1 carrot, cut into julienne strips (see page 147)
1 tsp sugar
10 tiger shrimp, cooked and peeled
5 small lettuce leaves
½ cup (15g) cilantro, separated into leaves
10 sheets of rice paper
20 mint leaves

FOR SAUCE

2 tbsp hoisin sauce
2 tbsp smooth peanut butter
1 tbsp tomato ketchup
5 tbsp water

Combine carrot strips with sugar and toss to coat each piece well. Let stand until wilted, 15 minutes.
Cut shrimp in half lengthwise. Cut lettuce leaves into 2in x 1in (5cm x 2.5cm) strips. Divide carrots and cilantror into 20 equal-sized portions. Set aside.
Pour about ¾in (1.5cm) cold water into a shallow dish. Dip 1 sheet of rice paper into the water and leave to soften, 2 minutes. Remove and spread out on a dry dish towel. Cut in half.
Top 1 half sheet with 1 lettuce strip, 1 mint leaf and 1 portion each of carrots and cilantro. Roll rice paper over to enclose filling. Fold both ends of rice paper over the enclosed filling. Place 1 shrimp half, cut side down, on top (see below, left). Continue rolling up into a cylinder and press the end with a wet finger to seal. Place the roll, seal side down, on a tray and cover with a dampened dish towel to keep moist. Repeat with the remaining half sheet rice paper, then start again with remaining rice paper sheets and filling.
For sauce, combine hoisin, peanut butter, ketchup, and water. Serve rice paper rolls chilled or at room temperature with peanut hoisin dipping sauce.

THINK AHEAD
Prepare filling ingredients up to 1 day in advance. Cover and refrigerate. Make rolls up to 3 hours in advance. Cover with a dampened dish towel and refrigerate. Be sure to keep the dish towel moist.

SUSHI RICE

MAKES 2 CUPS (300G)

1 cup (175g) short-grained rice
1 cup (200gz) water
½ cup (125ml) rice vinegar
5 tbsp sugar

In a large bowl, cover rice with cold water, stir it until the water turns cloudy. Pour off water. Repeat this 1 or 2 more times until water is almost clear. Drain rice in a strainer. Put drained rice in a pan, add 1 cup (200g) water, cover, and bring to a boil over a high heat. Boil for 2 minutes. Reduce heat to low and simmer until water is absorbed and rice is tender, 15 minutes. Remove from heat and let stand without lifting the lid, for 5 minutes.
In separate pan, bring vinegar and sugar to boil over medium heat, stirring until the sugar dissolves. Remove from heat and cool.
Turn the hot cooked rice out on to an oven tray and immediately drizzle the vinegar and sugar mixture evenly over the rice. Toss gently but thoroughly with a wooden spoon. Quickly cool the rice to room temperature by fanning it while continuing to toss the rice. Cover the rice with a dampened dish towel and cool completely.

THINK AHEAD
Make rice up to 3 hours in advance. Store covered with a dampened dish towel at room temperature.

COOKS' NOTE
Fanning the rice as it cools will make the rice especially glossy. Use a piece of stiff cardboard or a baking sheet if you don't have a fan.

CUCUMBER NORI SUSHI ROLLS

MAKES 24

2 tsp sesame seeds
2 sheets of nori, halved
1 recipe sushi rice (see opposite)
½ tsp wasabi paste
½ cucumber, seeded and cut into julienne strips (see page 147)
2 tbsp pickled ginger
6 tbsp shoyu (japanese soy sauce)
ESSENTIAL EQUIPMENT *bamboo sushi mat*

Toast seeds in a dry pan over low heat until nutty and golden, 3 minutes. Cool. Have a small bowl of water ready for moistening your fingers. Place 1 half piece nori, smooth side down, on the mat. Moisten your fingers with water, then spread a quarter of the rice in an even layer on the nori, leaving a ½in (1cm) strip uncovered at the end furthest away from you. Press down the rice with moistened fingers to pack firmly. Spread a thin line of wasabi lengthwise along the centre of the rice with your finger. Arrange a quarter of the cucumber, sesame seeds and ginger on top, making sure the fillings extend completely to each end of the rice. Pick up the bamboo mat and tightly roll rice around the filling, pulling the mat as you roll (see opposite). Unroll mat. Repeat with remaining nori, rice, wasabi, cucumber, sesame seeds and ginger. Cut each nori roll into 6 equal-sized pieces with a moist knife. Serve chilled or at room temperature with soy sauce for dipping.
THINK AHEAD
Make but do not cut nori rolls up to 1 day in advance. Store wrapped in plastic wrap at room temperature.

SMOKED SALMON SUSHI RICE BALLS

MAKES 20

¼lb (100g) smoked salmon slices
1 recipe sushi rice (see opposite)
1 tsp wasabi paste

Cut salmon into 20 - 1in (2.5cm) squares. Divide the rice into 20 equal-sized portions. Cut cling film into 20 - 4in (10cm) squares. Place 1 piece of salmon in the center of 1 plastic wrap square. Place 1 portion of rice on top. Gather cling film around the rice and twist the ends to make a tight ball (see below, right). Repeat with remaining salmon, plastic wrap and rice. Unwrap rice balls. Garnish with a knife's tip of wasabi. Serve chilled or at room temperature

THINK AHEAD
Make rice balls up to 2 days in advance. Refrigerate wrapped. Garnish up to 1 hour before serving.

SUSHI RICE BALL VARIATIONS

SALMON CAVIAR SUSHI RICE BALLS

Omit smoked salmon. Replace wasabi garnish with ¼lb (100g) salmon caviar. Wrap rice in plastic wrap as directed to make rice balls. Garnish each rice ball with 1 tsp salmon caviar up to 1 hour before serving.

SHRIMP SUSHI RICE BALLS

Substitute smoked salmon with 10 cooked, peeled tiger shrimp cut in half lengthwise. Place 1 shrimp half cut side up on each piece of plastic wrap. Top with rice and wrap in cling film as directed to make rice balls. Garnish with wasabi as directed.

THINK AHEAD
Make rice balls up to 2 days in advance. Refrigerate wrapped. Garnish up to 1 hour before serving.

Pull mat as you roll.

Twist to make tight balls.

MINI CALIFORNIA ROLLS

MAKES 40

5 sheets of nori
1 recipe sushi rice (see page 89)
½ cucumber, seeded and cut into julienne strips (see page 147)
1 avocado, finely sliced into 40 pieces
40 pickled ginger slices
1 tsp wasabi

ESSENTIAL EQUIPMENT
bamboo sushi mat

Fold nori sheets into three, lengthwise, to make a strip. Fold the strip into 3. Unfold and tear along the folded lines to make squares. Place the squares smooth side down. Have a small bowl of water ready for moistening your fingers. Place 1 half, smooth side down, on the mat. Divide the rice and cucumber into 40 equal-sized portions. Moisten your fingers with water, then spread 1 rice portion in an even layer over the left half of 1 nori square. Spread a thin line of wasabi lengthwise along the center of the rice with your finger. Arrange 1 portion cucumber, 1 avocado slice, and 1 ginger piece on top. Starting at the left corner, roll up the nori square like a cone, moistening with a wet finger to stick the nori together (see below, left).
Repeat with remaining nori, rice, wasabi, cucumber, avocado, and ginger. Serve at room temperature.

THINK AHEAD
Assemble up to 1 hour in advance. Cover with plastic wrap and store at room temperature.

SESAME SUSHI ROLLS

MAKES 24

3 tbsp sesame seeds
¼lb (125g) medium shrimp
2 sheets of nori, halved
1 recipe sushi rice (see page 89)
½ tsp wasabi paste

½ cucumber, seeded and cut into julienne strips (see page 147)
6 tbsp shoyu (japanese soy sauce)

ESSENTIAL EQUIPMENT
bamboo sushi mat

Toast seeds in a dry pan over low heat until nutty and golden, 3 minutes. Cool. Cut shrimp in half lengthwise.
Have a small bowl of water ready for moistening your fingers. Cut 1 sheet of plastic wrap just larger than 1 nori half. Place 1 nori half, smooth side down, on the mat. Moisten your fingers with water; then spread a quarter of the rice in an even layer on the nori. Cover with the plastic wrap. Pick up the nori, carefully turn over and place on the mat plastic wrap side down. The nori should now be facing up. Spread a thin line of wasabi lengthwise along the center of the nori with your finger. Arrange a quarter of the shrimp, cucumber and 1tsp sesame seeds on top, making sure the fillings extend completely to each end. Pick up the bamboo mat and plastic wrap and tightly roll rice around the filling, pressing down firmly as you roll. Unroll mat and plastic wrap. Gently roll the rice roll in half the remaining sesame seeds (see opposite, center). Roll up tightly in plastic wrap, twisting the ends to secure (see opposite, right). Repeat with remaining nori, rice, wasabi, shrimp, cucumber, and sesame seeds. Trim the ends of each roll to neaten, then cut each rice roll into 6 equal-sized pieces with a moist knife. Remove plastic wrap from the cut pieces. Serve at room temperature with shoyu for dipping.

THINK AHEAD
Assemble but do not cut rice rolls up to 1 day in advance. Store wrapped in plastic wrap at room temperature. Cut when ready to serve.

COOKS' NOTE
We used a mixture of black and brown sesame seeds for coating the roll that is pictured here. To make black sesame seeds, toast the seeds in a dry pan over a medium heat until blackened. For an alternative coating, try 2 tbsp red lumpfish roe.

WONTON WRAPPERS

MAKES 20

1¼ cups (150g) all-purpose flour
½ cup (125ml) boiling water

ESSENTIAL EQUIPMENT
2in (5cm) plain pastry cutter

Place the flour in a bowl and make a well in the center. Pour in the water. Mix with a fork to form a rough dough. Cover with a dish towel and let stand until cool enough to handle. Knead on a lightly floured surface until smooth and elastic, 5 minutes. Cover with a dish towel and let rest for 30 minutes. Roll out dough on a lightly floured surface to a ⅛in (0.25cm) thickness. Cut out 20 rounds with the pastry cutter.

THINK AHEAD
Make up to 1 day in advance. Store in an airtight container stacked in single layers separated by waxed paper. Alternatively, freeze wrappers up to 1 month in advance. Store in a sealed plastic freezer bag stacked in single layers separated by plastic wrap (see page 149). Defrost overnight in the refrigerator.

CRISPY WONTON CRESCENTS WITH GINGERED PORK AND CHILI SOY DIPPING SAUCE

MAKES 20

2½ oz (75g) lean ground pork
1 garlic clove, crushed
1 scallion, chopped
¾ in (2cm) piece ginger, grated
1 tbsp dark soy sauce
1 tsp sesame oil
1 recipe wonton wrappers, or 20 ready made round dumpling wrappers
2 tbsp all-purpose four for dusting
2 tbsp sunflower oil
1 cup (250ml) cold water for cooking

FOR SAUCE

1 tbsp chinese hot chili sauce
4 tbsp dark soy sauce

ESSENTIAL EQUIPMENT
wok with a lid

Place pork, garlic, scallion, ginger, soy sauce, and sesame oil in a food processor or blender; pulse until well combined. Place ½ tsp pork filling in the center of each wrapper. Fold wrapper over to enclose filling to make crescents. Press edges together to seal. With fingertips, crimp edges (see page 86). Dip the bottom of each wonton crescent in a little flour. Place on a floured baking pan and cover with a damp dish towel.
For sauce, combine chili sauce and soy sauce.
Heat 1 tbsp oil in the wok over medium heat. When oil is very hot, add half the wonton crescents flat-side down to the wok in a single layer. Cook until crispy underneath, 5 minutes. Add to the center of the wok enough water to come about halfway up the sides of each wonton crescent. Cover wok with the lid and cook until all the liquid has evaporated, 10 minutes. Remove wontons from wok; cover with foil and keep warm in a preheated 250°F (120°C) oven. Repeat with remaining oil, wonton crescents and water. Serve warm with chili soy dipping sauce.

THINK AHEAD
Assemble wonton crescents up to 3 hours in advance. Store covered with plastic wrap on a floured baking pan in the refrigerator. Alternatively, freeze (see page 149) up to 1 month in advance. Defrost overnight in the refrigerator. Fry up to 45 minutes before serving. Keep warm, covered in a preheated 250°F (120°C) oven.

COOKS' NOTE
It's the flour that makes the wonton crescents crispy. If assembling ahead of time, dip the wonton crescents again in flour before cooking for maximum crispiness.

CRISPY WONTON CRESCENT VARIATION

CRISPY WONTON CRESCENTS WITH HERBED PRAWN AND TANGY LIME DIPPING SAUCE

For herbed prawn filling, place 2½ oz (75g) cooked and peeled shrimp, 2 chopped scallions, 2 tbsp chopped cilantro, ½ in (1cm) piece ginger, grated, and 1 tbsp fish sauce in food processor or blender; pulse until finely chopped. Fill 1 recipe wonton wrappers or 20 ready made dumpling wrappers as directed by the main recipe. Fry crescents as directed by the main recipe.
For the tangy lime dipping sauce, combine juice of 1 lime with 1 tbsp sugar and 2 tbsp fish sauce. Serve wonton crescents warm with tangy lime dipping sauce.

TEXAS RED BEAN WRAPS WITH CILANTRO CREMA

MAKES 20

FOR BEAN FILLING

2 scallions

½ of a 15.5oz can (200g) of red kidney beans, drained

1 garlic clove, chopped

¼ tsp tabasco

juice of 1 lime

salt, black pepper

FOR CREMA

⅓ cup(75g) cream cheese

½ cup (15g) cilantro, chopped

1 green chili, seeded and chopped

½ tbsp olive oil

4 - 8in (20cm) flour tortillas

Roughly chop the white parts of the scallions. Reserve the green stalks for the crema. For bean filling, place chopped scallions, beans, garlic, tabasco and lime in a food processor or blender; process until well blended but still retaining some texture. Add salt and pepper to taste.

Roughly chop the reserved green stalks of the scallion. For crema, place chopped scallion stalks, cream cheese, chili, and oil in a food processor or blender; pulse until smooth.

Heat a dry heavy bottomed frying pan over medium heat. Place 1 tortilla in the pan. Cook until warm, 15 seconds. Flip tortilla over and warm other side, 15 seconds. Remove from pan and cover with a clean dish towel. Repeat with remaining tortillas.

Spread 1 warm tortilla first with 1 tbsp bean filling, then with 1 tbsp crema filling. Roll up tortilla gently, but firmly, as you would a jelly roll. Wrap securely in plastic wrap (see page 148). Twist the ends to secure. Repeat with remaining tortillas and filling. Refrigerate tortilla rolls 1 hour.

Trim untidy ends with a serrated knife. Cut each tortilla wrap diagonally into 5 slices. Discard the plastic wrap after slicing. Serve chilled or at room temperature.

THINK AHEAD

Make wraps up to 1 day in advance. Refrigerate. Slice up to 1 hour before serving. Discard the plastic wrap just before serving to keep tortilla wraps moist.

COOKS' NOTE

One word of wrap advice, do not overfill. If some filling does ooze out as you roll, simply scrape the excess off with the back of a knife.

ROASTED PEPPER, GOAT CHEESE AND MINT WRAPS

MAKES 20

1 red pepper, quartered and seeded

4 - 8in (20cm) flour tortillas

⅓ cup (75g) fresh creamy goat's cheese

½ cup(15g) mint, chopped

salt, black pepper

Broil and peel pepper quarters (see page 147). Cut peeled pepper quarters into julienne strips (see page 147).

Heat a dry heavy bottomed frying pan over medium heat. Place 1 tortilla in the pan. Cook until warm, 15 seconds. Flip tortilla over and warm other side, 15 seconds. Remove from pan and cover with a clean dish towel. Repeat with remaining tortillas.

Spread 1 warm tortilla with 1 tbsp goat's cheese. Top with a quarter of the pepper julienne strips. Sprinkle with mint and a pinch each salt and pepper. Roll up tortilla gently but firmly as you would a jelly roll. Wrap securely in plastic wrap (see page 148). Twist the ends to secure. Repeat with remaining tortillas and filling. Refrigerate tortilla rolls 1 hour.

Trim untidy ends with a serrated knife. Cut each tortilla wrap diagonally into 5 slices. Discard the plastic wrap after slicing. Serve chilled or at room temperature.

THINK AHEAD

Make wraps up to 4 hours in advance. Refrigerate. Slice up to 1 hour before serving. Discard plastic wrap just before serving to keep tortilla wraps moist.

CREPES

MAKES 5

½ cup (60g) all-purpose flour

¼ tsp salt

1 egg, beaten

⅔ cup (150ml) milk

2 tbsp (30g) butter

ESSENTIAL EQUIPMENT

9in (23cm) non-stick frying pan

Sift flour and salt into a bowl. Make a well in the center and add the eggs. Gradually beat in flour from the sides. Beating constantly, slowly pour in the milk to make a smooth batter. Cover and let stand at room temperature for 30 minutes.

Melt butter in the pan over medium heat. Swirl butter to coat the bottom of the pan. Pour excess melted butter into a bowl and reserve.

Pour a small ladle of batter into the pan. Tilt the pan and swirl the batter to cover the entire base of the pan. Cook until golden underneath, 1 minute. Flip crepe over with a rubber spatula and cook until golden underneath, 30 seconds more. Remove from pan. Repeat with reserved butter and remaining batter. Discard any thick or torn crepes.

THINK AHEAD

Make crepes up to 2 days in advance. Store in an airtight container stacked in single layers separated by waxed paper. Alternatively, freeze crepes up to 1 month in advance. Store in a sealed plastic freezer bag stacked in single layers separated by plastic wrap (see page 149). Defrost overnight in refrigerator.

COOKS' NOTE

Be sure to add the milk gradually while beating constantly in order to achieve a perfectly smooth batter. If lumps do occur, pour the batter through a strainer. Alternatively, make batter in a food processor or blender; process flour, salt, eggs, and milk until smooth.

ROLLED SMOKED HAM CREPES WITH TARRAGON AND MUSTARD CREAM

MAKES 20

½ cup (125g) cream cheese

1 tbsp grainy mustard

1 tbsp roughly chopped tarragon leaves

salt, black pepper

1 recipe crepes (see opposite)

5 slices smoked ham

Combine cream cheese, mustard, and tarragon. Add salt and pepper to taste. Spread crepes with cheese mixture. Roll up each ham slice tightly. Place 1 tightly rolled ham slice along the edge of 1 crepe. Roll crepe firmly around ham. Wrap in plastic wrap. Twist the ends to secure. Repeat with remaining filling, ham, and crepes. Refrigerate rolls 1 hour. Trim untidy ends with a serrated knife. Cut each rolled crepe into 4 slices, alternating between diagonal and straight cuts. Discard the plastic wrap after slicing. Serve chilled or at room temperature.

THINK AHEAD

Make rolled crepes up to 1 day in advance. Refrigerate. Cut up to 1 hour before serving.

ROLLED RICOTTA AND SAGE CREPES WITH PARMESAN SHAVINGS

MAKES 20

FOR CREPES

½ cup (60g) all-purpose flour

¼ tsp salt

1 egg, separated

1 cup (250ml) milk

1 tbsp melted butter

1 tbsp finely chopped sage

FOR FILLING

1 cup (200g) ricotta cheese

1 tbsp finely chopped sage

1 tbsp finely chopped parsley

1 tbsp grated parmesan cheese

salt, black pepper, nutmeg

4 tbsp (60g) butter

20 parmesan shavings to garnish (see page 148)

For crepes, place flour, salt, egg yolk, milk, butter, and sage with a pinch of salt in a food processor or blender; pulse until smooth. Beat egg white until soft peaks form (see page 141). Fold a third of the batter into the beaten egg white until lightened. Fold in remaining batter until well combined. Cover and refrigerate for 30 minutes.

For filling, combine ricotta, herbs, and parmesan until well combined. Add salt, pepper and nutmeg to taste.

Melt butter in the pan over a medium heat. Swirl butter to coat the bottom of the pan. Pour excess melted butter into a bowl and reserve. Pour a small ladle of batter into the pan. Tilt the pan and swirl the batter to cover the entire bottom of the pan. Cook until golden underneath, 1 minute. Flip crepe over with a rubber spatula and cook until golden underneath, 30 seconds more. Remove from pan. Repeat with reserved butter and remaining batter until used up. Discard any thick or torn crepes. Cool crepes completely. Spread ricotta mixture evenly over crepes. Roll up tightly (see page 148). Wrap in plastic wrap. Twist the ends to secure. Refrigerate rolls 1 hour. Trim untidy ends with a serrated knife. Cut each rolled crepe into 4 slices. Discard the plastic wrap after slicing. Garnish with parmesan shavings. Serve chilled or at room temperature.

THINK AHEAD

Roll crepes up to 1 day in advance. Cover and refrigerate. Cut and garnish up to 1 hour before serving.

MINI PEKING DUCK PANCAKES WITH PLUM SAUCE

MAKES 20

1 tsp honey
1 tsp light soy sauce
1 duck breast, skinned
1½ in (4cm) piece fresh ginger
2 scallions
½ cucumber, halved and seeded
20 long chives
10 ready made chinese pancakes
2 tbsp plum sauce

Preheat oven to 400°F (200°C) .
Combine honey and soy. Brush duck with honey soy mixture. Roast duck until browned but still pink and juicy inside, 10 minutes. Cool. Slice duck breast diagonally into ¼ in (0.5cm) thick slices.
Cut ginger, scallions, and cucumber in to julienne strips (see page 147). Drop chives into a pan of boiling water. Drain immediately and cool in cold water. Drain and pat dry with kitchen paper.
Cut pancakes in half. Trim a ¼ in (0.5cm) strip from the round edge of each pancake half to make 20 straight sided pieces. Spread ¼ tsp plum sauce in center of each piece. Divide duck slices and julienne strips among pancake strips. Roll up tightly and tie with a chive. Serve at room temperature.

THINK AHEAD
Roast duck breast up to 1 day in advance. Cover and refrigerate. Cut vegetables and blanch chives up to 1 day in advance. Store in an airtight container in the refrigerator. Slice duck and roll pancakes up to 1 hour in advance.

CHIVE-TIED CREPE BUNDLES WITH SMOKED SALMON AND LEMON CREME FRAICHE

MAKES 20

20 long chives
1 recipe crepes (see page 93)
grated peel of 1 lemon
½ cup (125ml) crème fraîche
8oz (250g) smoked salmon slices, chopped
2 tbsp finely chopped chives
black pepper

ESSENTIAL EQUIPMENT
3¼ in (8.5cm) plain pastry cutter

Drop long chives into a pan of boiling water. Drain and rinse immediately under cold water. Pat dry on kitchen paper. Cut out 4 rounds from each crepe with the pastry cutter. Combine lemon peel and crème fraîche. Place 1 tsp crème fraîche and 1 tsp smoked salmon in the centerof each crepe round. Sprinkle with chives and a pinch of black pepper. Carefully bring the edges of each crepe together into a little bundle. Tie each bundle with a long chive. Refrigerate until chilled, 15 minutes.

THINK AHEAD
Make crepe bundles up to 4 hours in advance. Store in single layers covered with plastic wrap in the refrigerator.

COOKS' NOTE
To make classic beggars' purses, omit chopped chives and pepper and substitute crème fraîche for sour cream and salmon for black caviar.

HERBED ARTICHOKE AND PARMESAN FILO ROLLS WITH LIGHT LEMON MAYONNAISE DIP

MAKES 20

8oz (250g) artichoke hearts in oil, drained

1 cup (100g) parmesan cheese, grated

1 egg, beaten

2 tbsp finely chopped parsley

2 tbsp finely chopped oregano

2 garlic cloves, crushed

¼ tsp salt

¼ tsp black pepper

8 sheets (200g) filo pastry

3 tbsp (45g) butter, melted

1 recipe light lemon mayonnaise (see page 142)

Preheat oven to 350°F (180°C).

For filling, place artichokes, cheese, egg, chopped herbs, garlic, salt, and pepper in food processor; pulse until blended. Brush butter on both sides of 3 filo sheets and stack them together. If necessary, trim stacked filo sheets to measure 6in (15cm) in width. Spread 1½ tsp of filling in a thin strip along the short end of the stacked filo. Roll the filo 1½ times around the filling (see below). Brush with butter to seal. Cut along the edge of the roll with a sharp knife to finish. Place the filo roll seam-side down on a buttered baking sheet. Repeat the rolling process with the remaining filling and butter to make about 5 or 6 rolls per filo stack. Layer and butter a new stack of filo sheets when you no longer have room to start a new roll. Repeat buttering and layering with the remaining filo sheets, spreading and rolling with the remaining filling until you have run out of ingredients. Brush finished filo rolls with more butter. Bake until crisp and golden, 15 minutes. Cool on a wire rack. Serve at warm or at room temperature with light lemon mayonnaise for dipping.

THINK AHEAD
Assemble up to 1 day in advance. Store covered in single layers not touching. Alternatively, assemble rolls and freeze up to 1 month in advance (see page 149) . Bake from frozen, 20-25 minutes.

COOKS' NOTE
If allowed to dry out, filo pastry becomes brittle and difficult to handle, so be sure to cover with a damp dish towel until ready to use.

MINTED FETA AND PINE NUT FILO ROLLS WITH LEMON AIOLI

MAKES 20

¾ cup (100g) pine nuts

¾ cup (100g) feta cheese, crumbled

2 tbsp grated parmesan cheese

2 tbsp finely chopped mint

grated peel of ½ lemon

1 tbsp lemon juice

¼ tsp black pepper

2 tbsp (30g) butter, melted

4 sheets (100g) filo pastry

1 recipe lemon aioli (see page 142)

Preheat oven to 350°F (180°C).

For filling, toast pine nuts in a dry pan over a low heat until nutty and golden, 5 minutes. Cool. Place pinenuts, feta, parmesan, mint, lemon peel, lemom juice, and pepper in a food processor; pulse until well blended.

Brush butter on both sides of 3 filo sheets and stack them together. If necessary, trim stacked filo sheets to measure 6in (15cm) in width. Spread 2 tsp filling in a thin strip along the short end of the stacked filo. Roll the filo 1½ times around the filling. Brush with butter to seal. Cut along the edge of the roll with a sharp knife to finish; then cut the finished roll in half. Place the 2 filo rolls seam-side down on a buttered baking sheet. Repeat the rolling process with the remaining filling and butter to make about 10 or 12 rolls per filo stack. Layer and butter a new stack of filo sheets when you no longer have room to start a new roll. Repeat buttering and layering with the remaining filo sheets, spreading and rolling with the remaining filling until you have run out of ingredients.

Brush filo rolls with butter. Bake until crisp and golden, 15 minutes. Cool on a wire rack. Serve at warm or at room temperature, with lemon aioli for dipping.

THINK AHEAD
Assemble up to 1 day in advance. Store covered in single layers not touching and refrigerate. Alternatively, assemble rolls and freeze up to 1 month in advance (see page 149). Bake from frozen, 20-25 minutes.

STACKS & CASES

FILO TARTLETS

MAKES 20
4oz package (75g) filo pastry
2 tbsp melted butter
ESSENTIAL EQUIPMENT
pastry brush, 2 - 12-cup mini muffin pans

Preheat oven to 350°F (180°C). Brush one sheet of filo pastry with the melted butter (see opposite, top). With a sharp knife cut into 2in x 2in (5cm x 5cm) squares (see opposite, middle). Butter the muffin cups and line each one with 4 buttered filo pastry squares placed at slightly different angles (see opposite, bottom). Repeat until all the filo pastry has been used. Bake to a deep golden brown, 6 to 8 minutes. Carefully remove the tartlets from the cups and let them cool completely on a wire rack.

THINK AHEAD
Bake tartlets up to 1 month in advance. Store in an airtight container at room temperature.

COOKS' NOTE
To prevent the filo pastry from drying out, cover with a damp cloth until ready to use. If the buttered filo sticks to your fingers, use the pastry brush to press the filo squares into the muffin cups.

FILO TARTLETS WITH BANG BANG CHICKEN

MAKES 20
2 tbsp sesame seeds
4 tbsp smooth peanut butter
1 garlic clove, crushed
2in (5cm) piece fresh ginger, chopped
2 tbsp lemon juice
1 tbsp dark soy sauce
¼ tsp tabasco
1 boneless, skinless chicken breast half
1 recipe filo tartlets (see above)
1 scallion, finely sliced on the diagonal (see below, right), to garnish

Preheat oven to 350°F (180°C).
Toast sesame seeds in a dry pan over low heat until nutty and golden, 3 minutes. To make bang bang sauce, mix peanut butter, garlic, ginger, lemon, soy sauce, and tabasco until smooth.
Put chicken in pan and cover with cold water. Bring slowly to simmering point. Simmer gently without boiling until cooked through, 7 to 10 minutes. Cool completely in cooking liquid. Drain and cut chicken on the diagonal into ⅛in (0.25cm) thick slices. Cut slices in half. Place 1 tsp bang bang sauce in each tartlet. Arrange chicken slices on top. Sprinkle with toasted seeds.
Garnish with scallion slices.

THINK AHEAD
Make sauce up to 3 days in advance. Cover and refrigerate. Cook chicken up to 1 day in advance. Cover and refrigerate. Fill tartlets up to 45 minutes before serving.

SLICING SCALLION
Trim scallion at both ends. Finely slice green stem at an angle to make sharp spikes.

FILO TARTLETS WITH SMOKED SALMON, CRACKED PEPPER, AND LIME

MAKES 20

5oz (150g) smoked salmon, thinly sliced
1 lime, peeled and segmented (see page 147), to garnish
½ cup (125ml) crème fraîche
1 recipe filo tartlets (see page 98)
juice of 1 lime
½ tsp cracked black peppercorns
½ cup (15g) chives, cut into ¾in (2cm) strips, to garnish

Cut salmon slices into thin strips, ¼in (0.5cm) wide. Cut lime segments into ½in (1cm) pieces. Place 1 tsp crème fraîche in bottom of each tartlet. Top with smoked salmon strips. Spoon over a few drops of lime juice and sprinkle with cracked black pepper. Garnish with lime segments and chive strips.

THINK AHEAD
Fill tartlets up to 45 minutes before serving.

COOKS' NOTE
You can buy cracked black pepper, but it is easy to make yourself. Crush the peppercorns with a mortar and pestle until cracked to tiny pieces rather than ground to a powder.

FILO TARTLETS WITH SMOKED CHICKEN, BLACK OLIVES, AND PARSLEY PESTO

MAKES 20

1 cup (15g) parsley
1 clove garlic, crushed
4 tbsp pine nuts
4 tbsp parmesan cheese, grated
juice of ½ lemon
2 tbsp olive oil
salt, black pepper
1 smoked chicken breast
1 recipe filo tartlets (see page 98)
10 pitted black olives, halved

Place parsley, garlic, pine nuts, parmesan, lemon juice, and oil in a food processor or blender; pulse to a thick paste. Add salt and pepper to taste. Cut chicken into thin strips, ¼in (0.5cm) wide. Put 1 tsp pesto into each tartlet. Arrange chicken strips on top. Garnish with half an olive. Serve at room temperature.

THINK AHEAD
Make pesto up to 3 days in advance. Cover and refrigerate. Fill tartlets up to 45 minutes before serving.

FILO TARTLETS WITH CRAB, GINGER, AND LIME

MAKES 20

1 tbsp sesame seeds
¾ lb (250g) crab meat
1in (2.5cm) piece fresh ginger,
finely chopped
juice of 2 limes
½ cup (15g) cilantro, leaves stripped
¼ red pepper, cut into strips
4 tbsp mayonnaise (see page 142)
salt, tabasco
1 recipe filo tartlets (see page 98)
1 lime, peeled and segmented
(see page 147), to garnish

Toast seeds in a dry pan over low heat
until golden brown, 3 minutes. Toss crab
with ginger, lime juice, cilantro, pepper,
mayonnaise, and toasted seeds. Add salt
and tabasco to taste. Cut lime segments
into ½in (1cm) pieces. Divide crab
among filo tartlets. Garnish with lime
segments. Serve at room temperature.

THINK AHEAD
Make filling up to 1 day in advance but add
coriander only up to 1 hour before serving.

FILO TARTLETS WITH SPICY CILANTRO SHRIMP

MAKES 20

2 tsp sesame seeds
¼lb (125g) medium shrimp, cooked,
peeled, and chopped
½ cup (15g) cilantro, finely chopped
6 tbsp thai sweet chili sauce
1 recipe filo tartlets (see page 98)

Toast seeds in a dry pan over low heat
until golden brown, 3 minutes. Combine
shrimp, cilantro, and chili sauce. Spoon
into tartlets and garnish with toasted
seeds.

THINK AHEAD
Make filling up to 1 day in advance. Cover and
refrigerate. Fill tartlets up to 45 minutes before
serving.

COOKS' NOTE
If using frozen cooked shrimp, defrost in a colander.
When defrosted, squeeze out water with your hands
and pat dry with paper towels.

FILO TARTLETS WITH ASIAN BEEF SALAD

MAKES 20

½lb (200g) beef fillet steak, 1in (2.5cm)
thick
1 tbsp light soy sauce
1 tbsp lime juice
1 tbsp fish sauce
¼ tsp sugar
½ cup (15g) cilantro, leaves stripped
½ cup (15g) mint, leaves stripped
¼ red pepper, finely diced
1 tomato, seeded and diced (see page 147)
1 tsp sesame seeds
1 tsp grated lime peel
1 recipe filo tartlets (see page 98)
1 sliced red chili to garnish

Sear steak in hot pan on both sides,
6 minutes in total. Cool and cut into
20 slices. Toss steak slices with soy
sauce, lime juice, fish sauce, sugar, fresh
herbs, pepper, tomato, seeds, and lime
peel. Divide steak slices among filo
tartlets. Garnish with red chili.

THINK AHEAD
Make filling up to 1 day in advance, but add fresh
herbs only up to 1 hour before serving. Cover and
refrigerate. Fill tartlets up to 45 minutes before
serving.

CORN CUPS

MAKES 20

⅔ cup (125g) masa harina

½ tsp salt

⅔ cup (150ml) warm water

ESSENTIAL EQUIPMENT

2½ in (6.5cm) plain pastry cutter;
2 - 12-cup mini muffin pans

Preheat oven to 400°F (200°C).
Place masa harina and salt in a bowl.
Pour in water and mix with a fork to
form a rough dough. Turn out onto a
clean surface and knead until smooth
and firm, 1 minute. Roll into a
smooth ball, cover with a dish towel,
and let rest for 30 minutes.
Cut dough in half. Roll out 1 piece of
dough between 2 pieces of plastic
wrap to a ⅛ in (3mm) thickness. Peel
off the top layer of plastic wrap. Cut
out 10 rounds with the pastry cutter.
Line 10 greased muffin cups with the
rounds. Repeat with remaining
dough and muffin cups. Bake until
crisp and dry, 20 minutes. Cool on a
wire rack.

THINK AHEAD
Bake cups up to 3 days in advance. Store in an
airtight container at room temperature.

COOKS' NOTE
Corn dough is an easy dough to work with. If the
dough tears slightly as you line the muffin cups,
simply fill the hole with a scrap of dough.

CORN CUPS WITH PAPAYA, AVOCADO, AND PINK GRAPEFRUIT SALAD

MAKES 20

½ pink grapefruit, peeled and segmented
(see page 147)

½ papaya

½ red onion, finely chopped

1 red chili, seeded and finely chopped

2 tbsp finely chopped mint

1 tbsp red wine vinegar

2 tbsp sunflower oil

1 small avocado, quartered

salt, black pepper

1 recipe corn cups (see opposite)

Cut each grapefruit segment into
½ in (1cm) pieces. Cut papaya half into
quarters. Cut each papaya quarter into
fine slices. Combine grapefruit, papaya,
onion, chili, mint, vinegar, and oil. Cut
each avocado quarter into fine slices.
Add to salad and gently combine. Add
salt and pepper to taste. Divide among
corn cups. Serve chilled or at room
temperature.

THINK AHEAD
Make salad up to 8 hours in advance, but add mint no
more than 3 hours in advance for best color. Press
plastic wrap directly onto the surface of the salad and
refrigerate. Fill corn cups just before serving.

CORN CUPS WITH TUNA, MANGO, AND LIME CEVICHE

MAKES 20

⅓ lb (175g) fresh tuna

juice of 2 limes

1 green chili, seeded and finely diced

½ medium red onion, finely chopped

1 mango, finely diced

2 tbsp finely chopped cilantro

1 tsp salt

1 recipe corn cups (see opposite)

Finely dice tuna. Combine tuna and lime
juice in a non-metallic bowl. Cover and
refrigerate, stirring occasionally, for 3
hours. Drain, discarding all but 1 tbsp
marinade. Combine tuna, chili, onion,
mango, cilantro, salt, and reserved
1 tbsp marinade. Divide among corn
cups. Serve chilled.

THINK AHEAD
Make ceviche up to 1 day in advance, but add
cilantro not more than 3 hours before serving for best
color. Cover and refrigerate. Fill corn cups just before
serving.

COOKS' NOTE
Fresh salmon, halibut, and scallops all make excellent
ceviche. If you are uncomfortable about serving raw
fish, use cooked, peeled shrimp instead.

BACON-WRAPPED OYSTERS

MAKES 20
20 fresh oysters
½lb (200g) bacon
1½ tbsp worcestershire sauce
20 tbsp coarse salt

ESSENTIAL EQUIPMENT
20 wooden toothpicks

Preheat oven to 400°F (200°C).
Open the oysters (see below), reserving
20 bottom shells for serving.
Cut bacon slices across into 20 strips, each
1¾in (4cm) long. Wrap a bacon strip around
each oyster and secure with a toothpick.
Place wrapped oysters on a baking
sheet. Bake until bacon is lightly colored
and cooked through, 10 minutes.
Arrange oysters on reserved shells. To
make a stable base for serving the
oyster, place each half shell on 1 tbsp of
coarse salt. Sprinkle oysters with
worcestershire sauce. Serve hot.

THINK AHEAD
Wrap oysters in bacon up to 2 hours in advance.
Cover and refrigerate.

OPENING OYSTERS
Hold oyster flat side up in a
dish towel. Insert a short,
wide-bladed kitchen or oyster
knife into hinge of the oyster
and twist to pry shell open.
Scrape oyster free from top
shell. Slice under flesh to
detach oyster from bottom
shell.

MUSSELS WITH SALSA CRUDA

MAKES 20
20 large fresh mussels
6 tbsp coarse sea salt
2 tomatoes, peeled, seeded, and diced
(see page 147)
1 green chili, seeded and finely chopped
½ medium red onion, finely chopped
2 tbsp olive oil
1 tbsp lime juice
salt, black pepper

Scrub mussels under running water.
Discard any that are broken or not
tightly closed. Pull off their beards with
your fingers. Place mussels in a pan
with 2 tbsp water and cover with lid.
Steam over medium heat until open,
6 minutes. Shake pan occasionally to
ensure even cooking. Remove mussels
with a slotted spoon. Discard any that
are shut. Cool. Pry open with your
fingers. Discard top shells. Loosen
mussels from bottom shells. Sprinkle
serving dish evenly with coarse salt.
Arrange mussels in half shells on salt.
For salsa, combine tomatoes, chili,
onion, oil, and lime juice. Add salt and
pepper to taste. Spoon over mussels.
Serve at room temperature or chilled.

THINK AHEAD
Cook mussels up to 1 day in advance. Cover and
refrigerate. Make salsa up to 5 hours in advance.
Cover and refrigerate. Top mussels up to 30 minutes
before serving.

CLAMS WITH GINGER AND LIME BUTTER

MAKES 20
6 tbsp (90g) butter, softened
½in (1cm) piece fresh ginger,
finely chopped
grated peel and juice of 1 lime
1 tbsp finely chopped cilantro
salt, black pepper
20 clams, littleneck, or other small hard
shell
6 tbsp coarse salt

Combine butter, ginger, lime peel and
juice, and cilantro. Add salt and pepper
to taste.
Scrub clams under running water.
Discard any that are broken or not
tightly closed.
Place clams in a pan with 2 tbsp water
and cover with lid. Steam over medium
heat until open, 6 minutes. Shake pan
occasionally to ensure even cooking.
Remove clams with a slotted spoon.
Discard any that are shut. Cool. Pry
open with your fingers. Discard top
shells. Loosen clams from bottom shells.
Sprinkle a heatproof serving dish evenly
with salt. Arrange half shells on salt.
Divide butter among clams. Before
serving, place clams under a preheated
broiler until butter melts, 2 minutes.
Serve hot.

THINK AHEAD
Make butter up to 1 week in advance. Cover and
refrigerate. Cook clams up to 1 day in advance. Cover
and refrigerate. Top clams with butter up to 1 hour in
advance. Broil and serve hot.

COOKS' NOTE
To barbecue clams, place unopened on a grill rack
6in (15cm) above hot coals. When the shells open,
the clams are done, 5 minutes. Discard top shell.
Have the ginger and lime butter already melted and
drizzle over the cooked clams. Cool slightly before
serving or you might burn your fingers.

EGG AND BACON PUFFS

MAKES 35

½lb (200g) bacon
1 hardboiled egg, halved
4 tbsp mayonnaise (see page 142)
½ cup (15g) chives, finely sliced
salt, black pepper
1 recipe baked choux puffs
(see pages 138-139)

Preheat oven to 350°F (180°C).
Place bacon on a foil-lined
baking sheet. Bake until golden and
crisp, about 10 to15 minutes. Drain
bacon on paper towels; then cut into
small
dice. Separate egg yolk from white.
Finely dice egg white. Crush yolk with
fork. Combine bacon, egg white,
mayonnaise, and chives (reserving 2 tsp
chives for garnish). Add salt and pepper
to taste. Cut ¼in (0.5cm) slice from the
top of each puff with a serrated knife.
Spoon egg and bacon mixture into puffs.
Sprinkle with egg yolk. Garnish with
chives. Serve at room temperature
or chilled.

THINK AHEAD
Make filling up to 1 day in advance. Cover and refrig-
erate. Fill puffs up to 3 hours in advance. Refrigerate.
Garnish up to 45 minutes before serving.

CLASSIC SHRIMP COCKTAIL PUFFS

MAKES 35

½lb (200g) small shrimp, cooked and
peeled
3 tbsp mayonnaise (see page 142)
1 tbsp tomato ketchup
1 tsp worcestershire sauce
salt, tabasco
1 recipe baked choux puffs
(see pages 138-139)
2 small bibb lettuces or romaine hearts,
separated into leaves
paprika for dusting

Combine shrimp, mayonnaise, ketchup,
and worcestershire sauce. Add salt and
tabasco to taste. Cut ¼in (0.5cm) slice
from top of each puff with a serrated
knife. Cut stalks from salad leaves and
discard. Cut each leaf into 1in (2.5cm)
pieces. Tuck one lettuce piece into each
puff. Spoon shrimp mixture on top.
Dust with paprika. Serve at room
temperature or chilled.

THINK AHEAD
Make filling up to 1 day in advance. Cover and refrig-
erate. Fill puffs up to 3 hours in advance. Refrigerate.
Garnish up to 45 minutes before serving.

LIGHT LEMONY SALMON MOUSSE PUFFS

MAKES 35

½lb (200g) salmon fillet
2 tbsp cream cheese
2 tsp horseradish sauce
2 tsp lemon juice
salt, white pepper
⅔ cup (150ml) heavy cream
1 recipe baked choux puffs
(see pages 138-139)
3½ oz (100g) salmon caviar
35 dill sprigs to garnish

ESSENTIAL EQUIPMENT
piping bag with large star nozzle

Place salmon in pan of boiling water.
When water returns to a boil, remove
from heat at once. Leave salmon in
water to cool completely. Drain on
paper towels. Place salmon with cream
cheese, horseradish, and lemon juice in a
food processor or blender; pulse until
smooth. Be careful not to overmix. Add
salt and pepper to taste. Whip cream
until it holds soft peaks (see page 144).
Gently fold salmon mixture into cream.
Cut ¼in (0.5cm) slice from the top of
each puff using a serrated knife. Fill
piping bag with mousse (see page 146).
Pipe mousse into puffs. Garnish with
salmon caviar and dill sprigs. Serve
chilled or at room temperature.

THINK AHEAD
Make filling up to 3 hours in advance. Cover and
refrigerate. Fill and garnish up to 1 hour in advance.

CARAMEL PROFITEROLES

MAKES 35

4 tbsp sugar

2 tbsp water

1 pint (500ml) vanilla ice cream

1 recipe baked choux puffs (see pages 138-139)

ESSENTIAL EQUIPMENT

baking sheet lined with greased baking parchment, melon baller

Put sugar and water in small pan and stir to dissolve. Bring to a boil over medium heat. Cook to a light caramel (see page 145 and below, left). Dip each puff in caramel (see below, right). Place puffs dipped-side down on the prepared baking sheet. Allow the caramel to set. Cut each dipped choux in half with a serrated knife.

With melon ball cutter, scoop 1 ball of ice cream. Sandwich the ice cream ball between 2 halves of 1 choux puff. Repeat with remaining ice cream and puffs. Serve immediately.

THINK AHEAD

Dip puffs up to 3 hours in advance.

MINI ECLAIRS

MAKES 30

1 recipe baked choux mini éclairs (see pages 138-139)

1 recipe chocolate pastry cream (see page 145)

3½ oz (100g) semisweet chocolate

Pierce a small hole in underside of each éclair. Fill piping bag with pastry cream (see page 146). Pipe cream into pierced hole in each éclair (see below, left). Melt chocolate (see page 145). Remove from hot water. Hold the bottom of each éclair between finger and thumb. Dip each éclair's upper surface into the chocolate. Remove quickly and allow excess chocolate to drip off (see below, right). Place on a wire rack, until chocolate is set. Serve cold or at room temperature.

THINK AHEAD

Fill and dip up to 1 day in advance. Cover and refrigerate. Alternatively, bake and freeze mini choux éclairs up to 3 weeks in advance. Crisp from frozen in preheated 350°F (180°C) oven for 3 minutes. Cool completely before filling.

COOK TO A LIGHT CARAMEL

DIP EACH PUFF IN CARAMEL

FILLING ECLAIRS

DIPPING ECLAIRS

CROUSTADES

MAKES 20
7 thin slices white bread
2 tbsp melted butter

ESSENTIAL EQUIPMENT
1 rolling pin, 1 - 2in (5cm) fluted pastry cutter, 2 - 12-cup muffin pans

Preheat oven to 400°F (200°C). Roll out bread slices thinly with the rolling pin. Cut out 3 rounds from each slice using the pastry cutter. Line each hole of 1 muffin pan with a bread round. Brush each round with butter. Press the empty muffin pan on top. Bake until golden brown and crisp, 10 minutes. Repeat with remaining bread.

THINK AHEAD
Make up to 3 days in advance. Store in an airtight container at room temperature.

COOKS' NOTE
Put your pasta machine to unusual but most efficacious use by rolling out the bread in it. Set machine on the third setting and roll the bread slices through twice. Cut out rounds according to the recipe.

MINI CAESAR SALAD CROUSTADES

MAKES 20
2 romaine hearts, leaves separated
2 tbsp mayonnaise (see page 142)
dash of worcestershire sauce
squeeze of lemon juice
5 drained anchovy fillets, finely chopped
1 tbsp parmesan cheese, grated
1 recipe croustades (see opposite)
20 parmesan shavings to garnish (see page 148)

Stack salad leaves and roll up tightly. Slice across roll to make ¼in (0.5cm) strips. Flavor mayonnaise with worcestershire sauce and lemon juice. Toss salad with mayonnaise, anchovies, and grated parmesan. Fill croustades with salad. Garnish with parmesan shavings.

THINK AHEAD
Prepare salad leaves up to 1 day in advance. Store in an airtight container in the refrigerator. Fill croustades up to 1 hour before serving.

TOMATO CONCASSEE WITH CREME FRAICHE AND CHIVES CROUSTADES

MAKES 20
3 ripe tomatoes, peeled, seeded, and diced (see page 147)
2 tbsp finely chopped chives
2 tbsp crème fraîche
2 tbsp lemon juice
tabasco
salt, black pepper
1 recipe croustades (see opposite)

Combine tomatoes with chives, crème fraîche, lemon juice, and a dash of tabasco. Cover and refrigerate for 1 hour. Add salt and pepper to taste. Spoon concassée into croustades. Serve cold.

THINK AHEAD
Make concassée the day before, but add salt and pepper only just before using. Store in an airtight container in the refrigerator. Fill croustades up to 45 minutes before serving.

POACHED SALMON WITH DILL MAYONNAISE CROUSTADES

MAKES 20
⅔ lb (300g) salmon fillet
1 recipe croustades (see page 108)
salt, white pepper
6 tbsp mayonnaise (see page 142)
2 tbsp finely chopped dill
20 dill sprigs to garnish

Place salmon in pan of boiling water. When water returns to a boil, remove from heat at once and let cool completely. Drain salmon on paper towels. Separate into large flakes. Divide salmon among croustades. Sprinkle with salt and white pepper. Combine mayonnaise and dill. Spoon mayonnaise over salmon. Garnish with dill sprigs. Serve at room temperature.

THINK AHEAD
Cook salmon up to 3 days in advance. Cover and refrigerate. Fill croustades up to 45 minutes before serving.

COOKS' NOTE
Use very finely chopped cilantro and a squeeze of lime in place of dill to create a subtle asian flavor.

QUAIL EGG, CAVIAR, AND CHERVIL CROUSTADES

MAKES 20
10 quail eggs
6 tbsp mayonnaise (see page 142)
1 recipe croustades (see page 108)
3½ oz (100g) black lumpfish caviar
3½ oz (100g) red lumpfish caviar
20 sprigs of chervil or parsley to garnish

Cook quail eggs in pan of boiling water for 5 minutes. Drain and refresh in cold water. Peel and cut in half. Spoon mayonnaise into croustades. Place half a quail egg cut side up on top of the mayonnaise. Top with ½ tsp each black and red caviar. Garnish with herb sprigs. Serve at room temperature.

THINK AHEAD
Cook and peel eggs up to 2 days in advance. Cover with water and refrigerate. Fill croustades up to 45 minutes before serving.

COOKS' NOTE
As an alternative filling, try lemon hollandaise (see page 143), crispy crumbled bacon, and snipped chives.

USING A ZESTER
Press down lightly, drag or pull the zester across the lemon rind.

CHICKEN TONNATO WITH LEMON AND CAPERS CROUSTADES

MAKES 20
1 boneless, skinless chicken breast half
2 tbsp drained tuna
2 drained anchovy fillets
2 tbsp mayonnaise (see page 142)
1 tsp lemon juice
salt, black pepper
1 recipe croustades (see page 108)
20 drained capers
peel of ½ lemon to garnish (see below)
ESSENTIAL EQUIPMENT
zester

Put chicken in pan with cold water to cover. Bring slowly to a simmer over medium-low heat. Simmer gently without boiling until cooked through, 7 to 10 minutes. Cool completely in cooking liquid. Drain and finely dice chicken. For tonnato sauce, place tuna, anchovies, mayonnaise, and lemon juice in a food processor; pulse until smooth. Add salt and pepper to taste. Divide chicken among croustades. Spoon over sauce. Garnish with capers and lemon peel. Serve at room temperature.

THINK AHEAD
Make tonnato sauce up to 3 days in advance. Cover and refrigerate. Cook chicken up to 1 day in advance. Cover and refrigerate. Fill croustades up to 45 minutes before serving.

CARROT, HONEY, AND GINGER SOUP CUPS

MAKES 20

2 tbsp (30g) butter
6 cups (750g) carrots, chopped
1 onion, chopped
1 garlic clove, chopped
4in (10cm) piece fresh ginger, chopped
3 celery sticks, chopped
salt, black pepper
1 quart (1 liter) chicken stock
1 tbsp honey
4 tbsp heavy cream
1 tbsp chopped chives to garnish

ESSENTIAL EQUIPMENT
20 espresso or demi-tasse cups

Melt butter in a pan over low heat. Add carrots, onion, garlic, ginger, and celery with a pinch of salt. Continue cooking, covered, until very soft, 20 minutes. Add stock and increase heat to boil. Reduce heat and simmer until carrots are cooked through, 15 minutes. Cool slightly, then place in a food processor or blender; pulse to a smooth purée. Place a fine-mesh strainer over the rinsed-out pan and press the purée through. Discard remainder left behind. Add 2 tbsp (30ml) water to the purée at a time to adjust the soup's thickness to the consistency of light cream. Heat soup through over medium heat. Add honey, cream, salt, and pepper to taste. Ladle into cups. Sprinkle with chives to garnish. Serve hot.

THINK AHEAD
Make up to 2 days in advance. Cover and refrigerate.

COOK'S NOTE
Remember that this soup will be sipped from a cup and not served with a spoon. Add water as specified by the recipe to achieve the proper consistency for this.

CHILLED SPICED CHICKPEA SOUP CUPS WITH AVOCADO SALSA

MAKES 20

FOR SOUP
14½oz (400g) can of chickpeas, drained
14½oz (400g) can of tomatoes
½ cup (125ml) whole-milk yogurt
2 garlic cloves, crushed
1 tsp ground cumin
1 tbsp lemon juice
2 tbsp olive oil
salt, cayenne pepper

FOR SALSA
1 medium avocado
½ medium red onion, finely chopped
1 tbsp finely chopped mint
1 tbsp lemon juice
1 tbsp olive oil
salt, black pepper
6 tbsp whole-milk yogurt

ESSENTIAL EQUIPMENT
20 espresso or demi-tasse cups

For soup, place chickpeas, tomatoes, yogurt, garlic, cumin, lemon juice, and oil in a food processor or blender; pulse to a smooth purée. Transfer purée to a bowl. Gradually add up to ½ cup (125ml) water to adjust the soup's thickness to a sipping consistency. Add salt and pepper to taste. Cover and refrigerate for 30 minutes to allow flavors to blend.
For salsa, finely dice avocado. Combine avocado, onion, mint, lemon juice, and oil. Add salt and pepper to taste. Cover and refrigerate for 15 minutes to allow flavors to blend.
Ladle soup into cups. Top with 1 tsp each salsa and sour cream. Serve chilled.

THINK AHEAD
Make soup up to 2 days in advance. Cover and refrigerate. Make salsa up to 8 hours in advance. Cover tightly with plastic wrap and refrigerate.

COOKS' NOTE
To help keep the salsa from discoloring when making it in advance, press a piece of plastic wrap directly onto the surface of the salsa. The oxygen in the air will turn peeled avocado brown, so the less air that contacts the salsa, the longer it will look fresh.

FOCACCINE FARCITE WITH BLUE CHEESE AND ARUGULA

MAKES 20
1 recipe unbaked bread dough
(see page 140)
1 cup (125g) gorgonzola cheese, crumbled
½ bunch (15g) arugula leaves
2 tomatoes, seeded and diced
(see page 147)
salt, black pepper
1 tbsp olive oil

ESSENTIAL EQUIPMENT
2in (5cm) plain pastry cutter

Preheat oven to 400°F (200°C).
Roll out dough to a ⅛in (0.25cm) thickness. Cut out 40 rounds with the pastry cutter. Place 20 dough rounds on a floured baking sheet. Top each focaccina with 1 tsp cheese, 2 arugula leaves, and ½ tsp diced tomato. Sprinkle with salt and pepper. Place remaining dough rounds on top. Press edges down to seal. Dimple focaccine with your fingertips. Bake until crisp and golden, 15 minutes. Brush with olive oil and serve warm.

THINK AHEAD
Bake focaccine up to 1 day in advance. Store in an airtight container. Crisp for 10 minutes in preheated 400°F (200°C) oven and serve warm. Freeze unbaked (see page 149) for up to 1 month in advance. Bake from frozen in preheated 400°F (200°C) oven for 20 minutes.

FOCACCINE FARCITE WITH WILD MUSHROOMS AND THYME

MAKES 20
1 tbsp olive oil
2 shallots, finely chopped
3½oz (100g) wild mushrooms, roughly chopped
1 tsp finely chopped thyme
salt, black pepper
1 recipe unbaked bread dough
(see page 140)
1 tsp coarse salt
3 thyme sprigs, roughly chopped

ESSENTIAL EQUIPMENT
2in (5cm) plain pastry cutter

Preheat oven to 400°F (200°C).
Heat oil in a frying pan. Add shallots and mushrooms. Stir fry over high heat until softened, 5 minutes. Add chopped thyme and salt and pepper to taste. Cool completely.
Roll out dough to a ⅛in (0.25cm) thickness. Cut out 40 rounds with pastry cutter. Place 20 dough rounds onto a floured baking sheet. Spoon wild mushrooms onto rounds. Top with remaining dough rounds. Press edges down to seal. Sprinkle with coarse salt. Bake until crisp and golden, 15 minutes. Garnish with thyme sprigs and serve warm.

THINK AHEAD
Bake focaccine up to 1 day in advance. Store in an airtight container. Crisp for 10 minutes in preheated 400°F (200°C) oven. Freeze unbaked (see page 149)

FOCACCINE FARCITE WITH RAISINS, FENNEL, AND GRAPES

MAKES 20
½ cup (100g) raisins
1 recipe unbaked bread dough
(see page 140)
30 black or red grapes, halved
2 tbsp fennel seeds

ESSENTIAL EQUIPMENT
2in (5cm) plain pastry cutter

Preheat oven to 400°F (200°C).
Pour boiling water to cover over raisins and let them soak until plump, 30 minutes. Drain and discard water.
Roll out dough to a ⅛in (0.25cm) thickness. Cut out 40 rounds with the pastry cutter. Place 20 dough rounds on a floured baking sheet. Cover with raisins and top with remaining dough rounds. Press edges down to seal. Top each focaccina with 3 grape halves and sprinkle with fennel seeds. Bake until crisp and golden, 15 minutes. Serve warm.

THINK AHEAD
Bake focaccine up to 1 day in advance. Store in an airtight container. Crisp for 10 minutes in preheated 400°F (200°C) oven and serve warm. Freeze unbaked (see page 149) for up to 1 month in advance. Bake from frozen in preheated 400°F (200°C) oven for 20 minutes.

MINI DOUBLE CHOCOLATE MERINGUE KISSES

MAKES 20
3½ oz (100g) semisweet chocolate
½ cup (100ml) heavy cream
1 tbsp sugar
1 recipe chocolate meringue kisses
(see page 141)
2 tsp cocoa powder for dusting

Melt chocolate (see page 145); cool.
Whip cream until it holds soft peaks.
Beat in sugar (see page 144). Hold 1
meringue by its pointed end and dip its
flat underside in chocolate; repeat with
another meringue. Sandwich two
prepared meringues together with 1 tsp
cream in between. Repeat with
remaining meringues. Dust with cocoa
powder. Serve at room temperature.

THINK AHEAD
Fill kisses up 2 hours in advance. Keep at room
temperature until ready to serve.

MINI RASPBERRY RIPPLE MERINGUE KISSES

MAKES 20
½ cup (100ml) heavy cream
1 tbsp sugar
1 cup (100g) raspberries
1 recipe vanilla meringue kisses
(see page 141)

Whip cream until it holds soft peaks.
Beat in sugar (see page 144). Crush
raspberries with fork and gently fold
into cream until cream is "rippled" with
raspberry color. Hold 1 meringue by its
pointed end and scoop up a little of the
raspberry cream on its flat underside;
repeat with another meringue. Sandwich
two prepared meringues together.
Repeat with remaining meringues.
Refrigerate for 30 minutes to set cream.
Serve chilled.

THINK AHEAD
Fill kisses up to 3 hours in advance. Cover and
refrigerate.

MINI LEMON MERINGUE KISSES

MAKES 20
½ cup (100ml) heavy cream
1 tbsp sugar
4 tbsp lemon curd
1 recipe vanilla meringue kisses
(see page 141)
2 tsp powdered sugar for dusting

Whip cream until it holds soft peaks.
Beat in sugar (see page 144). Fold lemon
curd into whipped cream. Hold 1
meringue by its pointed end and scoop
up a little of the lemon cream on its flat
underside; repeat with another meringue.
Sandwich two prepared meringues
together. Repeat with remaining
meringues. Refrigerate for 30 minutes to
set cream. Dust with powdered sugar to
garnish. Serve chilled.

THINK AHEAD
Fill kisses up to 3 hours in advance. Cover and
refrigerate. Dust with sugar just before serving.

MINI BURGER BUNS

MAKES 25

1 recipe unbaked bread dough
(see page 140)
1 egg yolk beaten with 1 tbsp water
1 tbsp sesame seeds

Preheat oven to 400°F (200°C).
Divide dough into small walnut-sized
pieces and shape into smooth rolls.
Place on a floured baking sheet and
press down gently to flatten to buns.
Cover with a cloth and leave for 20
minutes until doubled in size. Brush
each bun with beaten egg and
sprinkle with sesame seeds. Bake
until golden brown, 10 minutes.
Cool on a wire rack.

THINK AHEAD
Bake buns up to 3 days in advance. Store in an airtight container at room temperature. Alternatively,
shape and freeze buns. Bake frozen buns in preheated 400°F (200°C) oven for 20 minutes.

COOKS' NOTE
No time for bread making? Buy full-size burger
buns and cut in half. Cut out rounds from each
half using a 1½ in (4cm) pastry cutter.

MINI HAMBURGERS WITH PICKLES AND KETCHUP

MAKES 25

⅔ lb (300g) ground beef
1 tbsp very finely chopped onion
2 tbsp worcestershire sauce
1 tsp dijon mustard
1 tsp salt, ¼ tsp black pepper
4 tbsp tomato ketchup
1 recipe mini burger buns, halved
(see opposite)
2 little gem lettuces or romaine hearts,
separated into leaves
10 cornichons, to garnish

Preheat oven to 400°F (200°C).
Mix beef, onion, worcestershire sauce,
mustard, salt and pepper, and 1 tbsp
ketchup until well combined. Divide
mixture into 25 walnut-sized pieces.
With wet hands, shape pieces into balls
and flatten into burgers. Place on baking
sheet and cook until browned and firm
to the touch, 10 minutes. Cut stalks
from salad leaves and discard. Cut
leaves into 1in (2.5cm) pieces. Cut
cornichons on diagonal into thin slices.
Place burgers on bottom halves of
burger buns. Top with salad, cornichon
slices, and ketchup. Gently press on top
half of burger bun. Serve warm or at
room temperature.

THINK AHEAD
Cut buns up to 1 day in advance. Store in an airtight
container at room temperature. Shape burgers up to
1 day in advance. Cover and refrigerate. Assemble
burgers up to 3 hours in advance.

COOKS' NOTE
When shaping the burgers, make sure to flatten them
properly. If the mini burgers have a slightly domed
top, the burger buns will tend to topple off.

MINI TUNA BURGERS WITH WASABI MAYONNAISE AND PICKLED GINGER

MAKES 25

½ lb (250g) tuna steak, ⅝ in (1.5cm) thick
4 tbsp mayonnaise (see page 142)
1 tsp wasabi paste
¼ tsp soy sauce
¼ tsp rice vinegar
pinch sugar
25 pieces pickled ginger
25 cilantro leaves to garnish
1 recipe mini burger buns, halved
(see opposite)

ESSENTIAL EQUIPMENT
cast-iron grill pan.

Cut tuna into 1in (2.5cm) cubes.
Preheat pan over high heat. Sear tuna
cubes on both sides until firm to touch,
2 minutes per side. Add salt and pepper
to taste. Cool.
Combine mayonnaise, wasabi, soy sauce,
vinegar, and sugar. Divide mayonnaise
mixture among bottom bun halves. Top
with tuna pieces and garnish with ginger
and cilantro leaves. Cover with top bun
halves. Serve warm or at room
temperature.

THINK AHEAD
Cut buns up to 1 day in advance. Store in an airtight
container at room temperature. Assemble tuna
burgers up to 2 hours in advance.

COOKS' NOTE
Barbecue the tuna for the best flavor. Place tuna on an
oiled rack set 3in (7.5cm) above medium hot coals for
2 minutes on each side.

BASIC BOUCHEE RECIPE

MAKES 30

8oz (175g) puff pastry
1 egg yolk beaten with 1 tbsp water

ESSENTIAL EQUIPMENT
1¾in (4.5cm) fluted pastry cutter,
1in (2.5cm) fluted pastry cutter

Preheat oven to 400°F (200°C).
Roll out pastry to a ⅛in (3mm)
thickness. Cut out 60 rounds with the
large pastry cutter. With the small
cutter, cut out a circle from the
center of half of the pastry rounds
(see below, left). This results in 30
rounds and 30 rings. Brush the
pastry rounds with the beaten egg.
Place the rings on the rounds (see
below, right). Gently press to seal.
Place topped rounds on a floured
baking sheet. Brush again with
beaten egg. Bake until risen and
golden brown, 12 minutes. Cool on a
wire rack. Cool to room temperature
before filling.

THINK AHEAD
Bake up to 1 week in advance. Store in an airtight
container in a single layer at room temperature.

TARRAGON AND MUSTARD LOBSTER BOUCHEES

MAKES 30

¼lb (125g) cooked lobster meat, shredded
1 tomato, peeled, seeded, and diced
(see page 147)
2 tbsp sliced tarragon
1 tsp dijon mustard
4 tbsp mayonnaise (see page 142)
salt, black pepper
1 recipe baked bouchées (see opposite)

Combine lobster, tomato, tarragon,
mustard, and mayonnaise. Add salt and
pepper to taste. Use a teaspoon to fill
bouchées with lobster mixture. Serve at
room temperature.

THINK AHEAD
Make filling up to 1 day in advance. Cover and
refrigerate. Fill bouchées up to 30 minutes before
serving.

COOKS' NOTE
Chopped shrimp or white crab meat are both
delicious substitutes for the lobster in this recipe.

WILD MUSHROOM, GARLIC, AND THYME BOUCHEES

MAKES 30

1 tbsp (15g) butter
4oz (125g) wild mushrooms, finely
chopped
1 shallot, finely chopped
1 garlic clove, finely chopped
1 tsp finely chopped thyme
2 tbsp crème fraîche
salt, black pepper
1 recipe baked bouchées (see opposite)
30 thyme sprigs to garnish

Melt butter in a frying pan over high
heat. Add mushrooms, shallots, garlic,
and thyme. Stir fry until tender and
slightly crisp, 5-10 minutes. Stir in
crème fraîche and remove from heat.
Add salt and pepper to taste. Use a
teaspoon to fill bouchées with mushroom mixture. Garnish with thyme.
Serve hot or at room temperature.

THINK AHEAD
Make filling up to 1 day in advance. Cover and
refrigerate. Warm through gently over low heat with
1 tbsp extra crème fraîche. Fill bouchées up to 45
minutes in advance. Garnish just before serving.

WONTON CUPS

MAKES 20

1¼ cups (150g) all-purpose flour
½ cup (125ml) boiling water

ESSENTIAL EQUIPMENT
2 - 12-cup mini muffin pans

Place the flour in a bowl and make a well in the center. Pour in the water and mix with a fork to form a rough dough. Cover with a dish towel and let stand until cool enough to handle. Knead on a lightly floured surface until smooth and elastic, 5 minutes. Cover with a dish towel and let rest for 30 minutes.
Preheat oven to 400°F (200°C). Roll out dough on a lightly floured surface to a pape-thin thickness. With a sharp knife, cut into about 20 squares, 2in x 2in (5cm x 5cm) each. Grease the muffin cups of both pans and line each one with a wonton pastry square. Bake until crisp, 10 minutes. Cool before removing from tins.

THINK AHEAD
Make up to 2 weeks in advance. Store in an airtight container at room temperature.

SQUID, SESAME, AND LIME WONTON CUPS

MAKES 20
2 tsp sesame seeds
1 tbsp sesame oil
1 tbsp sunflower oil
grated peel of ½ lime
juice of 1 lime
1 tsp fish sauce
1 scallion, finely chopped
¼lb (150g) baby squid rings
1 recipe wonton cups (see opposite)

Toast seeds in a dry pan over low heat until nutty and golden, 3 minutes. Cool. Combine toasted seeds, oils, lime peel, fish sauce, and scallion; set aside. Bring a pan of water to a boil. Add the squid. When the water has returned to a boil, continue cooking for just 30 seconds. Drain and rinse under cold water. Dry on paper towels.
Add squid to sesame lime dressing and stir to coat each ring well. Divide among wonton cups. Serve chilled or at room temperature.

THINK AHEAD
Make squid, sesame, and lime salad up to 1 day in advance. Cover and refrigerate. Fill wonton cups up to 1 hour before serving.

FIVE-SPICE DUCK AND PAPAYA WONTON CUPS

MAKES 20
1 tsp honey
½ tsp five-spice powder
1 tsp dark soy sauce
1 duck breast, skinned
1 tsp rice wine vinegar
1 tsp sesame oil
1 tsp soy sauce
1 recipe wonton cups (see opposite)
½ papaya, diced
20 cilantro leaves to garnish

Preheat oven to 400°F (200°C). Combine honey, spice powder, and dark soy sauce. Brush duck on both sides with honey-soy mixture. Roast for 10 minutes. Cool completely. Cut across into very fine slices. Combine duck with vinegar, oils, and soy sauce. Stir to coat each slice well. Divide duck among wonton cups. Top with diced papaya and garnish with cilantro leaves.

THINK AHEAD
Cook and dress duck up to 1 day in advance. Cover and refrigerate. Dice papaya up to 1 day in advance. Cover and refrigerate. Fill wonton cups up to 1 hour in advance.

CUCUMBER CUPS WITH BLUE CHEESE MOUSSE AND CRISPY BACON

MAKES 20
6 slices bacon
4oz (125g) roquefort cheese
½ of 8oz package (125g) cream cheese
salt, black pepper
1 scallion, cut into strips, to garnish
1 recipe cucumber cups (see opposite)

ESSENTIAL EQUIPMENT
piping bag with large star nozzle

Preheat oven to 350°F (180°C). Place bacon on a foil-lined baking pan. Cook until golden and crisp, about 10to15 minutes. Drain on paper towels and cut into small triangular pieces. Beat cheeses until smoothly blended. Add salt and pepper to taste. Fill piping bag with mousse (see page 146) and pipe into cucumber cups. Top with crispy bacon pieces. Garnish with scallion strips.

THINK AHEAD
Prepare mousse up to 3 days in advance. Cover and refrigerate. Cook bacon up to 1 day in advance. Store in an airtight container in the refrigerator. Crisp in pre-heated 350°F (180°C) oven for 2 minutes. Fill cups up to 1 hour before serving.

CUCUMBER CUPS

MAKES 20
1 cucumber
ESSENTIAL EQUIPMENT
1⅜in (3.5cm) fluted pastry cutter; melon baller

Cut cucumber into 20 - ¾in (1.5cm) thick slices. Cut each slice with pastry cutter (see opposite, left). Using melon ball cutter, scoop out centers to make cups, leaving a ¼in (0.5cm) layer as a base (see opposite, right).

THINK AHEAD
Make cups up to 2 days in advance. Store in an airtight container in the refrigerator.

CUCUMBER CUPS WITH SMOKED TROUT MOUSSE, LEMON, AND DILL

MAKES 20
5oz (150g) smoked trout
4oz package (125g) cream cheese
½ tsp grated lemon peel
1 tbsp lemon juice
cayenne pepper
1 recipe cucumber cups (see above)
1 tsp paprika for dusting
20 dill sprigs to garnish

ESSENTIAL EQUIPMENT
piping bag with large star nozzle

Place smoked trout, cream cheese, peel, and juice in a food processor or blender; pulse to a smooth paste. Add cayenne pepper to taste. Fill piping bag with mousse (see page 146) and pipe into cucumber cups. Dust with paprika and garnish with dill sprigs.

THINK AHEAD
Make mousse up to 1 day in advance. Cover and refrigerate. Fill cups up to 1 hour before serving.

CUCUMBER BARQUETTES WITH SMOKED SALMON AND PICKLED GINGER

MAKES 20
3½oz (100g) smoked salmon slices
20 pieces of pickled ginger
1 tsp wasabi paste
20 cucumber barquettes (see below)

Cut salmon into 20 - ¼in (0.5cm) wide strips. Put a piece of ginger on top of each salmon strip and roll up. Put a dab of wasabi on each cucumber boat. Top with a smoked salmon roll.

THINK AHEAD
Fill barquettes up to 1 hour before serving.

MAKING BARQUETTES
Peel and cut cucumber in half. Cut each half into ¼ in (5cm) pieces. Use tip of knife to trim off ½ in (0.5cm) of flesh from the inside of each piece. Cut each piece into a diamond shape, about 2in (5cm) across.

CELERY BARQUETTES WITH STILTON AND WALNUTS

MAKES 20

8 large celery stalks
4oz (125g) stilton cheese
4oz package (125g) cream cheese
salt, black pepper
1 tsp paprika for dusting
20 walnut pieces to garnish

ESSENTIAL EQUIPMENT
piping bag with large star nozzle

Cut celery stalks on diagonal to make
20 - 2in x 2in (5cm x 5cm) diamond-
shaped pieces. Beat stilton and cream
cheese until well combined. Add salt and
pepper to taste. Fill piping bag with
cheese mixture (see page 146) and pipe
into celery barquettes. Dust with
paprika and garnish with walnuts.

THINK AHEAD
Make filling up to 2 days in advance. Cover and refrig-
erate. Prepare barquettes up to 2 days in advance.
Store in an airtight container in the refrigerator.
Fill barquettes up to 1 hour before serving.

CHERRY TOMATOES WITH CRAB AND TARRAGON MAYONNAISE

MAKES 20

20 cherry tomatoes
½lb (250g) crab meat
4 tbsp mayonnaise (see page 142)
1 tsp dijon mustard
1 tbsp tarragon leaves, sliced
salt, black pepper

Cut and discard thin slices from stalk
end of tomatoes to make flat, stable
bases. Cut and reserve thin slices from
smooth end to make tomato lids. Scoop
out seeds with teaspoon and discard.
Turn tomatoes upside down on paper
towels to drain for 5 minutes. Combine
crab, mayonnaise, mustard and
tarragon. Add salt and pepper to taste.
Use a teaspoon to fill tomatoes with crab
mixture. Top with tomato lids.

THINK AHEAD
Prepare tomatoes up to 2 days in advance. Store in an
airtight container in the refrigerator. Fill tomatoes up
to 3 hours before serving. Cover and refrigerate.

RADISH CUPS WITH BLACK OLIVE TAPENADE

MAKES 20

¼cup (150g) pitted black olives
4 anchovy fillets
2 tbsp capers
1 garlic clove, finely chopped
1 tsp lemon juice
1 tsp finely chopped thyme
2 tbsp olive oil
¼ tsp black pepper
20 round radishes

ESSENTIAL EQUIPMENT
melon ball cutter

Place olives, anchovies, capers, garlic,
lemon juice, thyme, and oil in a food
processor or blender; pulse to a thick
paste. Add pepper. Cut and discard thin
slices from radish bottoms to make flat,
stable bases. Cut and reserve thin slices
from radish tops to make radish lids.
Using melon ball cutter, remove most of
radish center to make "cups." Fill cups
with tapenade. Top with reserved
radish lids.

THINK AHEAD
Make filling up to 1 month in advance. Cover and
refrigerate. Prepare cups up to 2 days in advance.
Store in an airtight container in the refrigerator.
Fill cups up to 1 hour before serving.

COOKS' NOTE
If you don't have radishes with tops, a sprig of dill will
make a decorative and flavorful alternative garnish.

QUESADILLA TRIANGLES WITH SMOKY SHREDDED CHICKEN

MAKES 24

1 boneless, skinless chicken breast half
3 tbsp sunflower oil
½ medium onion, finely chopped
2 garlic cloves, crushed
½ tsp ground cumin
½ tsp ground coriander
1 canned chipotle pepper in adobo sauce (see page 162), chopped
7oz (200g) chopped tomatoes
1 tsp tomato purée
½ tsp sugar
salt, black pepper
6 - 6in (15cm) flour tortillas
6 tbsp grated gruyère cheese
2 scallions, finely chopped
⅓ cup (75ml) sour cream
24 cilantro leaves to garnish

ESSENTIAL EQUIPMENT
cast-iron grill pan

Place chicken in a pan with cold water to cover. Simmer gently over low heat, being careful not to boil, until cooked through, 7 to 10 minutes. Cool completely before draining. Drain and shred chicken.
Heat 2 tbsp oil in a skillet over medium heat. Stir fry onion until softened, 5 minutes. Add garlic, cumin, coriander, chili, tomatoes, tomato purée, and sugar. Cook until thickened, 5 minutes. Cool. Combine with shredded chicken. Add salt and pepper to taste. Preheat grill pan over medium heat. Brush 1 side of a tortilla with oil. Place oiled side down onto the pan, pressing lightly with a spatula. Pan grill, 1 minute. Repeat with remaining tortillas. Preheat oven to 400°F (200°C). Place half the tortillas on a baking sheet marked side down. Combine cheese and scallions. Sprinkle 1 tbsp cheese-onion mix; then 1 tbsp chicken over each tortilla. Sprinkle 1 tbsp cheese-onion mix over each topped tortilla. Top with remaining tortillas. Bake until cheese melts, 5 minutes. Cool slightly. Cut into 8 wedges with kitchen scissors or a serrated knife. Garnish triangles with sour cream and cilantro leaves. Serve warm or at room temperature.

THINK AHEAD
Make chicken up to 1 day in advance. Cover and refrigerate. Prepare tortillas and fill up to 1 hour before serving. Cover and keep at room temperature.

QUESADILLA TRIANGLES WITH HOT PEPPER RELISH

MAKES 24

6 - 6in (15cm) flour tortillas
1 tbsp sunflower oil
1 red pepper, quartered and seeded
2 green chilies, seeded and finely diced
½ garlic clove, crushed
1 tbsp olive oil
1 tbsp red wine vinegar
2 tbsp finely chopped cilantro
¼ tsp sugar
salt, black pepper
6 tbsp grated gruyère cheese
⅓ cup (75ml) sour cream
1 scallion to garnish

ESSENTIAL EQUIPMENT
cast-iron grill pan

Preheat grill pan over medium heat. Brush 1 side of a tortilla with oil. Place tortilla oiled side down onto the pan, pressing lightly with a spatula. Cook until grill marks show, 1 minute. Repeat with remaining tortillas.
For relish, broil and peel pepper quarters (see page 147). Finely chop broiled pepper. Combine pepper with chili, garlic, oil, vinegar, cilantro, and sugar. Add salt and pepper to taste. Cover and let stand for 1 hour at room temperature to allow the flavors to blend. Preheat oven to 400°F (200°C).
Place half the tortillas on a baking sheet. Sprinkle with 1 tbsp cheese; then spread 1 tbsp relish over each tortilla. Sprinkle with another 1 tbsp cheese. Top with remaining tortilla. Bake until cheese melts, 5 minutes. Cool slightly.
For garnish, cut scallion diagonally into ½ in (1cm) pieces. Cut each quesadilla into 8 wedges with kitchen scissors or a serrated knife. To garnish, top quesadilla triangles with sour cream and a piece of scallion. Serve warm or at room temperature.

THINK AHEAD
Make salsa up to 1 day in advance. Cover and refrigerate. Prepare tortillas and fill up to 1 hour before serving. Cover and keep at room temperature.

COOKS' NOTE
We recommend wearing rubber gloves when working with chilies. Capsaicin, the substance in chilies that makes them hot and spicy, can cause a painful burning sensation if brought into contact with eyes or sensitive skin.

MINI MUFFINS

MAKES 20
1½ cups (175g) all-purpose flour
1 tsp baking powder
1 tsp baking soda
¼ tsp salt
6 tbsp sugar
1 egg, beaten
½ cup (125ml) milk
3 tbsp melted butter

ESSENTIAL EQUIPMENT
2 - 12-cup mini muffin pans, buttered

Preheat oven to 375°F (190°C). Sift flour, baking powder, baking soda, and salt into a bowl. Make a well in the center. Add remaining ingredients, plus additional flavoring, if using. Gently fold everything together to make a wet batter. Spoon batter into 20 of the buttered muffin cups. Bake until golden brown and firm to the touch, 12 minutes. Turn out and cool completely on a wire rack.

THINK AHEAD
Bake muffins up to 1 day in advance. Store in an airtight container.

COOKS' NOTES
When flavored, these mini muffins are delicious enough to be served without a filling. Place in preheated 350°F (180°C) oven for 5 minutes before serving.

FLAVORED MUFFIN VARIATIONS

ORANGE MUFFINS
Add grated peel of 1 orange to ingredients.

ROSEMARY MUFFINS
Add 2 tsp finely chopped rosemary to ingredients.

ORANGE MUFFINS WITH SMOKED TURKEY AND CRANBERRY SAUCE

MAKES 20
1 recipe orange mini muffins
(see opposite)
4 tbsp cream cheese
5oz (150g) smoked turkey slices
4 tbsp cranberry sauce

Cut muffins in half. Spread each bottom half with cream cheese. Cut turkey slices into 20 - 1in (2.5cm) wide strips. Place 1 turkey strip onto each muffin. Spoon sauce on top. Cover with top half of muffin. Serve at room temperature.

THINK AHEAD
Fill muffins up to 3 hours before serving. Store at room temperature.

ROSEMARY MINI MUFFINS WITH SMOKED HAM AND PEACH RELISH

MAKES 20
1 recipe rosemary mini muffins
(see opposite)
1 peach, fresh or canned
1 tsp cider vinegar
4 tbsp cream cheese
5oz (150g) smoked ham slices

For relish, finely dice peach. Toss with vinegar. Cut muffins in half. Spread each bottom half with cream cheese. Cut ham slices into 20 - 1in (2.5cm) wide strips. Place 1 ham strip onto each muffin. Spoon peach relish on top. Cover with top half of muffin. Serve at room temperature.

THINK AHEAD
Fill muffins up to 3 hours before serving. Store at room temperature.

COOKS' NOTE
We highly recommend the combination of smoked duck and redcurrant jelly as an alternative filling for these flavorful rosemary mini muffins.

BABY BAGELS

MAKES 20

1 recipe unbaked bread dough
(see page 140)
1 egg yolk beaten with 1 tbsp water
2 tbsp poppy or sesame seeds

ESSENTIAL EQUIPMENT
slotted spoon

Preheat oven to 400°F (200°C).
Divide dough into 20 walnut-sized
pieces. Shape each piece into a ball.
Form each ball into a ring by
inserting a floured finger into the
center (see below). Work your finger
in a circle to stretch and widen the
hole. Bring a pan of water to a boil
over high heat; then reduce heat to
simmering. Working in batches, use
the slotted spoon to lower bagels into
the water. Boil until bagels rise to
surface, about 1 minute. Remove from
water to a greased baking sheet with
the slotted spoon. Repeat with
remaining bagels. Brush bagels with
beaten egg and sprinkle with seeds.
Bake until golden, 10 minutes.

THINK AHEAD
Bake bagels up to 3 days in advance. Store in an
airtight container. Freeze bagels up to 1 month in
advance.

**FORM EACH
BALL INTO A
RING**
Insert floured
finger into the
center. Work
finger in a circle
to widen the
hole.

BABY BAGELS WITH CREAM CHEESE, LOX, AND DILL

MAKES 20

1 recipe baby bagels (see opposite)
4oz package (125g) cream cheese
½lb (200g) smoked salmon
black pepper
20 dill sprigs

Slice bagels in half and toast lightly.
Spread bottom halves with cream
cheese. Top with salmon and dill and
sprinkle with pepper. Cover with top
halves. Serve at room temperature.

THINK AHEAD
Fill bagels up to 5 hours in advance. Cover and store
at room temperature.

BABY BAGELS WITH ROASTED RED ONION, GOAT CHEESE, AND CHIVES

MAKES 20

2 red onions, roughly chopped
1 tbsp olive oil
salt, black pepper
1 recipe baby bagels (see opposite)
½ cup (125g) fresh creamy goat cheese
½ cup (15g) chives, roughly chopped

Preheat oven to 400°F (200°C).
Toss onions with oil, salt, and pepper.
Roast onions until soft, 15 minutes.
Slice bagels in half and toast lightly.
Spread each bottom half with goat
cheese. Sprinkle with salt and pepper.
Top with red onions and chives. Cover
with top halves. Serve at room
temperature.

THINK AHEAD
Fill bagels up to 5 hours in advance. Cover and store
at room temperature.

CHOCOLATE CUPS WITH KIWI, RASPBERRY AND LIME MOUSSE

MAKES 20

4oz package (125g) cream cheese
juice and grated peel of 2 limes
¼ cup (60g) sugar
½ cup (125ml) heavy cream
20 bought mini chocolate cups
½ kiwi fruit, peeled, to garnish
10 raspberries, halved, to garnish

ESSENTIAL EQUIPMENT
piping bag with large star nozzle

Beat cream cheese with juice, peel, and sugar until smooth. Whip cream until it holds soft peaks (see page 144). Fold cream into cream cheese mixture. Fill piping bag with mousse and pipe into chocolate cups (see page 146).
Cut kiwi across into ¼in (0.5cm) slices. Cut each slice into eighths. Garnish with kiwi triangles and raspberry halves.

THINK AHEAD
Fill cups up to 1 day in advance. Cover and refrigerate. Garnish up to 1 hour before serving.

CHOCOLATE CUPS WITH WHITE CHOCOLATE MOUSSE

MAKES 20

½ cup (125ml) heavy cream
1 egg white
4oz (125g) white chocolate, melted (see page 145)
20 bought mini chocolate cups
2 tbsp white chocolate curls to garnish
1 tsp cocoa powder for dusting

Whip cream until it holds soft peaks (see page 144). Beat egg white until it holds soft peaks. Fold melted chocolate into beaten whites; then fold in the whipped cream. Spoon mousse into chocolate cups. Refrigerate until set, about 1 hour. Garnish with white chocolate curls and a dusting of cocoa.

THINK AHEAD
Fill cups up to 1 day in advance. Cover and refrigerate. Garnish up to 1 hour before serving.

COOKS NOTE
To make chocolate flakes, grate white chocolate over the fine grate side of a cheese grater. To prevent the chocolate flakes from melting in your fingers, refrigerate the piece of chocolate briefly before begin and hold the chocolate with a piece of wax paper as you grate. Use a teaspoon to sprinkle the flakes over each chocolate cup.

CHOCOLATE CUPS WITH MANGO AND MASCARPONE CREAM

MAKES 20

1 fresh mango, peeled and sliced (see page 163)
⅓ cup (125g) mascarpone cheese
juice of ½ lime
1 tbsp sugar
20 bought mini chocolate cups
20 tiny mint sprigs to garnish

ESSENTIAL EQUIPMENT
piping bag with large star nozzle

Place mango, mascarpone, lime juice, and sugar in a food processor; pulse to a smooth purée. Fill piping bag with the purée (see page 146). Pipe into chocolate cups. Garnish with mint sprigs.

THINK AHEAD
Fill cups up to 1 day in advance. Cover and refrigerate. Garnish up to 1 hour before serving.

CHOCOLATE CUPS WITH STRAWBERRIES AND ORANGE CREME FRAICHE

MAKES 20

⅔ cup (150ml) crème fraîche
grated peel of 1 orange
20 bought mini chocolate cups
5 strawberries, sliced, to garnish

Mix crème fraîche and orange peel together. Use a teaspoon to fill chocolate cups with orange crème fraîche. Garnish with strawberry slices.

THINK AHEAD
Fill cups up to 1 day in advance. Cover and refrigerate. Garnish up to 1 hour before serving.

SOBA NOODLES WITH SESAME GINGER VINAIGRETTE IN SPOONS

MAKES 20

½ lb (250g) soba noodles

1 tbsp pickled ginger, finely chopped

2 tsp chinese hot chili sauce

4 tbsp rice wine vinegar

4 tbsp dark soy sauce

4 tbsp sesame oil

6 tbsp sunflower oil

2 tbsp sesame seeds to garnish

ESSENTIAL EQUIPMENT

20 chinese or soup spoons

Bring a pan of water to a boil over medium heat and add the noodles. When the water returns to a boil, add 1 cup (250 ml) cold water. Continue cooking until water returns to a boil. Repeat this process 1 or 2 times until the noodles are tender to the bite, 5to7 minutes. Drain and cool noodles in cold water. Leave in the colander for 5 minutes to drain well.

Combine noodles, ginger, chili sauce, vinegar, soy sauce, and oils and stir to coat the noodles well.

Toast seeds in a dry pan over low heat until nutty and golden, 3 minutes. Divide noodles into 20 equal-sized portions. Twirl each noodle portion around a fork to make a nest. Transfer to spoons. Garnish with sesame seeds. Serve at room temperature.

THINK AHEAD

Cook and dress noodles in vinaigrette up to 1 day in advance. Cover and refrigerate. Return to room temperature before serving.

COOKS' NOTE

Adding cold water to the noodles as they cook checks overvigorous boiling to ensure that the noodles cook evenly.

FRAGRANT COCONUT SAFFRON SHRIMP IN SPOONS

MAKES 20

20 medium shrimp, peeled

1 lemon grass stalk

1 shallot, finely chopped

½ in (1cm) piece fresh ginger, grated

1 garlic clove, finely chopped

pinch ground coriander

pinch saffron

1 tbsp sunflower oil

⅓ cup (100ml) coconut milk

¼ tsp salt, ¼ tsp black pepper

ESSENTIAL EQUIPMENT

20 chinese or soup spoons

With a small sharp knife, cut each shrimp almost in half lengthwise, leaving the tail end attached (see below, right).

Remove and discard the tough outer skin from the lemon grass and finely chop.

In a non-metallic bowl, toss lemon grass, shallots, ginger, garlic, spices, oil, and shrimp together to coat each shrimp well. Cover and refrigerate for 1 hour.

Remove shrimp and place lemon grass mixture in a pan over low heat. Cook gently, stirring, until fragrant, 5 minutes. Add coconut milk, salt, and pepper. Bring slowly to a bowl over medium heat. Add shrimp and simmer gently until they turn pink and lose their transparency, 3 minutes. Arrange 1 shrimp in each spoon. Drizzle over a little of the sauce to coat. Serve warm.

COOKS' NOTE

For both of the recipes on this page choose spoons that sit well on a flat surface and are easy to pick up.

PASSION FRUIT CURD TARTLETS

MAKES 20

5 passion fruit, halved
juice of ½ lemon
4 tbsp sugar
4 tbsp (60g) butter
1 egg, beaten
1 recipe baked pastry tartlets
(see pages 136-137)
2 tsp powdered sugar for dusting

ESSENTIAL EQUIPMENT
small non-stick or heavy based saucepan

Scoop passion fruit pulp out of each half with a teaspoon. Combine passion fruit pulp, lemon, and sugar in the saucepan. Add butter and place over low heat. Stir occasionally, until the butter has melted. Place the egg in a bowl. Beat egg constantly, while gradually pouring in the hot passion fruit mixture, until well blended. Return mixture to the pan. Cook over low heat, stirring constantly, until thick and creamy, 10 minutes. Remove from the heat and continue stirring until cooled slightly. Cool completely. Divide curd among tartlets. Dust with powdered sugar to garnish. Serve chilled or at room temperature.

THINK AHEAD
Make curd up to 3 days in advance. Cover and refrigerate. Fill tartlets up to 1 hour before serving.

COOKS' NOTE
Make lime or pink grapefruit curd for a refreshing alternative. Use ⅔ cup (150ml) lime or pink grapefruit juice and 1 tsp grated lime or pink grapefruit peel instead of the passion fruit pulp and lemon juice.

CHERRY AND ALMOND FRANGIPANE TARTLETS

MAKES 20

2 tbsp (30g) butter, softened
2 tbsp sugar
¼ cup (30g) ground almonds
1 egg yolk
1 tbsp heavy cream
1 recipe baked pastry tartlets
(see pages 136-137)
20 cherries (about 1 cup [175g]), pitted
2 tsp powdered sugar for dusting

Preheat oven to 350°F (180°C). Combine butter, sugar, almonds, egg, and cream until well blended. Divide evenly among tartlets. Place 1 cherry on top of each tartlet. Bake until set and golden, 15 minutes. Cool completely. Dust with powdered sugar to garnish. Serve at room temperature.

THINK AHEAD
Bake filled tartlets up to 1 day in advance. Store in an airtight container at room temperature. Garnish just before serving.

COOKS' NOTE
Use canned sweet cherries when fresh cherries are out of season.

CITRUS GINGER CREAM TARTLETS

MAKES 20

grated peel and juice of 1 lime
grated peel and juice of 1 lemon
6 pieces preserved stem ginger or candied ginger, 1 piece chopped and 5 pieces sliced
5 tbsp heavy cream
¾ cup (175ml) sweetened condensed milk
1 recipe baked pastry tartlets
(see pages 136-137)

ESSENTIAL EQUIPMENT
piping bag fitted with large star nozzle

Place lime and lemon peels, chopped ginger, cream, and condensed milk in a food processor or blender; pulse until combined. With the machine running, slowly pour in the lime and lemon juices until blended. Transfer to a bowl. Cover and refrigerate until set, 1 hour. Fill piping bag and pipe filling into the tartlets (see page 146). Garnish with the ginger slices. Serve chilled or at room temperature.

THINK AHEAD
Fill tartlets up to 1 day in advance. Cover and refrigerate. Garnish up to 2 hours before serving.

SUMMER BERRY TARTLETS

1 recipe vanilla pastry cream (see page 144)
1 recipe baked pastry tartlets (see pages 136-137)
1 cup (200g) summer berries: raspberries, halved strawberries, blackberries, or blueberries
2 tsp powdered sugar for dusting

ESSENTIAL EQUIPMENT
piping bag with large star tip

Fill piping bag with pastry cream (see page 146). Pipe into tartlets. Arrange berries on top. Dust with powdered sugar. Serve at room temperature.

THINK AHEAD
Assemble tartlets up to 3 hours in advance. Keep at room temperature. Dust just before serving.

BITTERSWEET CHOCOLATE TARTLETS

MAKES 20
⅓ cup (75ml) heavy cream
1 egg yolk
2½ oz (75g) bittersweet chocolate, broken into pieces
1 recipe baked pastry tartlets (see pages 136-137)
1 tbsp cocoa for dusting

Bring cream to a boil. Beat boiling cream into the egg yolk in a separate bowl. Add chocolate and stir until melted and smooth. Allow to cool until slightly thickened, 30 minutes. Spoon into pastry tartlets. Let filling set at room temperature. Dust with cocoa. Serve chilled or at room temperature.

THINK AHEAD
Make filling and assemble tartlets up to 3 hours in advance. Cover and refrigerate. Dust just before serving.

COOK'S NOTE
The chocolate flavor in this recipe is unadulterated, so use the brand of chocolate you like best. More or less bitter, depending on your preference.

CARAMELIZED LEMON TARTLETS

MAKES 20
1 egg, beaten
2 tbsp sugar
2 tbsp lemon juice, about 1 lemon
grated peel of 1 lemon
2 tbsp heavy cream
1 recipe baked pastry tartlets (see pages 136-137)
2 tbsp sugar to caramelize

Preheat oven to 375°F (190°C).
Beat eggs and sugar together until sugar dissolves. Whisk in lemon juice, peel, and cream until just combined. Leave for 5 minutes. Skim any froth off the top. Pour lemon mixture into baked tartlets. Bake until only just set, 5 to 8 minutes. Cool to room temperature. Sprinkle tartlets with a thin layer of sugar. Place tartlets under a preheated broiler as close to the heat as possible until the sugar has colored, 1 to 2 minutes. Watch constantly to avoid burning. Serve at room temperature.

THINK AHEAD
Bake filled tartlets up to 1 day in advance. Cover and refrigerate. Caramelize tops up to 3 hours before serving.

ASIAN CHICKEN WITH SPICY PESTO TARTLETS

MAKES 20

1 boneless, skinless chicken breast half

2 tbsp light soy sauce

1 tbsp rice vinegar

1 tbsp sesame oil

1 tbsp sunflower oil

FOR PESTO

1 cup (15g) cilantro

10 mint leaves

1 green chili, seeded

1 scallion

1 tbsp roasted peanuts

1 tbsp sesame oil

1 recipe baked star-shaped sesame seed tartlets (see pages 136-137)

Place chicken in a pan and cover with cold water. Bring to simmering over low heat. Simmer gently without boiling until cooked through, 7 to 10 minutes. Cool completely in cooking liquid. Drain and shred chicken. Toss chicken with soy sauce, vinegar, and sesame and sunflower oils. Place cilantro, mint, chili, scallion, peanuts, and oil in a food processor or blender; pulse to thick paste. Fill tartlets with chicken and top with pesto. Serve at room temperature.

THINK AHEAD
Cook chicken up to 2 days in advance. Cover and refrigerate. Prepare pesto up to 3 days in advance. Cover and refrigerate. Fill tartlets up to 2 hours before serving.

RARE ROAST BEEF WITH GRAINY MUSTARD IN POPPY SEED TARTLETS

MAKES 20

½ lb (200g) rare roast beef slices

1 tbsp grainy mustard

6 tbsp crème fraîche

1 recipe baked star-shaped poppy seed tartlets (see pages 136-137)

20 tarragon sprigs to garnish

Cut beef slices into 1in (2.5cm) wide strips. Stir mustard into crème fraîche and divide among tartlets. Roll up beef slices and place on top of cream. Garnish with tarragon. Serve at room temperature.

THINK AHEAD
Make cream up to 1 day in advance. Fill tartlets up to 2 hours before serving.

SHRIMP WITH GINGER MAYONNAISE IN CILANTRO TARTLETS

MAKES 20

6 tbsp mayonnaise (see page 142)

1 tsp finely chopped ginger

½ tsp turmeric

½ lb (200g) medium shrimp, cooked, peeled, and chopped

salt, cayenne pepper

1 fresh red chili, seeded

1 recipe baked star-shaped cilantro tartlets (see pages 136-137)

20 cilantro leaves to garnish

Combine mayonnaise with ginger and turmeric. Add shrimp, then salt and pepper to taste. Cut chili into a very fine julienne strips (see page 147). Divide shrimp mixture among tartlets. Garnish with chili and cilantro leaves. Serve at room temperature.

THINK AHEAD
Make filling up to 1 day in advance. Cover and refrigerate. Fill tartlets up to 2 hours before serving.

FETA, OLIVE, AND ROSEMARY QUICHETTES

MAKES 20

½ cup (60g) feta cheese, crumbled
1 egg yolk
3 tbsp heavy cream
black pepper
5 pitted black olives, quartered
20 rosemary sprigs to garnish
1 recipe baked pastry tartlets
(see pages 136-137)

Preheat oven to 350°F (180°C).
Divide feta among tartlets. Beat egg and
cream together. Add pepper to taste.
Spoon egg mixture into tartlets. Top
with olive quarters and rosemary sprigs.
Bake until golden and set, 7 minutes.
Serve warm.

THINK AHEAD
Bake up to 2 days in advance. Store in an airtight
container in the refrigerator. Warm through in
preheated 300°F (150°C) oven for 10 minutes

BLUE CHEESE, MASCARPONE, AND RED ONION CONFIT QUICHETTES

MAKES 20

1 recipe baked rosemary tartlets
(see pages 136-137)
2 tbsp (30g) butter
1 medium red onion, finely sliced
¼ tsp salt
1 tbsp brown sugar
black pepper
½ cup (60g) gorgonzola cheese, crumbled
3 tbsp mascarpone cheese
1 egg yolk

Preheat oven to 350°F (180°C).
Melt butter in a frying pan. Stir in
onions. Sprinkle with salt and sugar.
Cook gently, stirring occasionally, until
soft and dark, 30 minutes. Add salt and
pepper to taste. Divide among baked
tartlet cases. Crumble gorgonzola over
tartlets. Beat mascarpone and egg until
combined. Spoon into tartlets. Bake
until golden, 7 minutes. Serve warm.

THINK AHEAD
Bake up to 2 days in advance. Store in an airtight
container in the refrigerator. Warm through in
preheated 300°F (150°C) oven for 10 minutes.

PORTOBELLO MUSHROOM AND HOLLANDAISE TARTLETS

MAKES 20

2 tbsp (30g) butter
1 shallot, finely chopped
½ lb (200g) portobello mushrooms,
chopped
1 tbsp cream cheese
2 tbsp lemon juice
salt, black pepper
1 recipe lemon hollandaise (see page 143)
1 recipe baked pastry tartlets
(see pages 136-137)
6 basil leaves, cut into chiffonade
(see below, right), to garnish

Preheat oven to 400°F (200°C).
Heat butter in a skillet. Add shallots and
mushrooms. Stir fry over high heat until
softened, 5 minutes. Cool slightly. Place
mushroom mixture, cream cheese, and
lemon juice in a food processor or
blender; pulse to a rough purée. Add
salt and pepper to taste. Divide
mushroom mixture among tartlets. Put 1
tsp hollandaise on top and heat through
in the oven for 5 minutes. Sprinkle with
basil. Serve warm.

THINK AHEAD
Make mushroom mixture up to 3 days in advance.
Cover and refrigerate. Fill tartlets up to 2 hours before
serving. Store at room temperature.

MAKING BASIL CHIFFONADE
Stack basil leaves and
roll them together
tightly. Slice across roll
to make very fine
strips.

EGG, CAPER, AND CRESS FINGER SANDWICHES

MAKES 30
4 medium eggs
1 tbsp finely chopped drained capers
1 cup (15g) watercress, finely chopped
4 tbsp mayonnaise
salt, black pepper
3 tbsp (45g) butter, softened
10 medium slices white bread

Place the eggs in a pan of cold water. Bring water to a boil; then reduce heat and simmer for 8 minutes. Drain and cool eggs completely in cold water. Shell and chop eggs. Combine eggs, capers, watercress, and mayonnaise. Add salt and pepper to taste. Spread butter, then egg mayonnaise evenly over 5 bread slices.
Top with remaining bread. Cut off crusts using a serrated knife and discard. Cut each sandwich in half, then cut each half into 3 fingers about 1½in (3.5cm) wide. Serve chilled or at room temperature.

THINK AHEAD
Make sandwiches up to 1 day in advance, but do not remove crusts or cut. Cover with plastic wrap and refrigerate. Cut sandwiches up to 3 hours in advance.

RARE ROAST BEEF AND HORSERADISH MAYONNAISE FINGER SANDWICHES

2 tbsp mayonnaise (see page 142)
2 tsp horseradish sauce
10 medium slices brown bread
⅓lb (150g) thinly sliced rare roast beef
3 tbsp (45g) butter, softened

Combine mayonnaise and horseradish. Spread 5 bread slices evenly with horseradish-mayonnaise mixture. Top with roast beef. Spread butter evenly over remaining bread slices. Top beef with bread slices buttered-side down. Cut off crusts using a serrated knife and discard. Cut each sandwich in half, then cut each half into 3 fingers about 1½in (3.5cm) wide. Serve chilled or at room temperature.

THINK AHEAD
Make sandwiches up to 1 day in advance, but do not remove crusts or cut. Cover and refrigerate. Cut sandwiches up to 3 hours in advance.

SMOKED SALMON AND CHIVE CREAM FINGER SANDWICHES

MAKES 30
6oz package (175g) cream cheese
½ cup (15g) chives, finely chopped
grated peel of ½ lemon
1 tbsp lemon juice
10 medium slices brown bread
½lb (200g) smoked salmon slices
black pepper
3 tbsp (45g) butter, softened

Combine cream cheese, chives, lemon peel, and lemon juice. Spread mixture evenly over 5 bread slices. Top with smoked salmon and sprinkle with black pepper. Spread butter evenly over remaining bread slices. Top salmon with bread slices buttered-side down. Cut off crusts using a serrated knife and discard. Cut each sandwich in half, then cut each half into 3 fingers about 1½in (3.5cm) wide. Serve chilled or at room temperature.

THINK AHEAD
Make sandwiches up to 1 day in advance, but do not remove crusts or cut. Cover with plastic wrap and refrigerate. Cut sandwiches up to 3 hours in advance.

AFTERNOON TEA CUCUMBER AND CHERVIL FINGER SANDWICHES

MAKES 30
½ cucumber, peeled and thinly sliced
½ tsp salt
6 tbsp (90g) butter, softened
10 medium slices white bread
white pepper
2 tbsp finely chopped chervil

Place cucumber slices in a colander. Sprinkle evenly with salt. Cover and let stand for 1 hour. Pat cucumber dry with paper towels.
Spread butter evenly over all bread slices. Top 5 bread slices with cucumber. Sprinkle with white pepper and chervil. Top cucumber with remaining bread slices. Cut off crusts using a serrated knife and discard. Cut each sandwich in half, then cut each half into 3 fingers about 1½in (3.5cm) wide. Serve chilled or at room temperature.

THINK AHEAD
Make sandwiches up to 8 hours in advance, but do not remove crusts or cut. Cover and refrigerate. Cut sandwiches up to 3 hours in advance.

MINI CROQUE MONSIEUR

MAKES 20
10 medium white bread slices
5 ham slices
7oz (200g) gruyère cheese, grated

Preheat oven to 400°F (200°C).
Top 5 bread slices with 1 slice ham each. Sprinkle half the cheese over the 5 slices. Press the remaining bread slices on top to make sandwiches. Place on a baking sheet. Sprinkle the remaining cheese across the top of the sandwiches. Bake until cheese is golden and melted, 10 minutes. Cool slightly. Cut off the crusts with a serrated knife. Cut each sandwich into 4 squares.
Serve warm.

CROQUE MONSIEUR VARIATION

MINI CROQUE MADAME

Use 3½oz (100g) gruyère cheese instead of 7oz (200g). Fill sandwiches as directed but do not top with cheese. Bake until bread is toasted, 10 minutes. Cut sandwiches as directed. Fry 20 quail eggs in 2 tbsp (30g) butter. Top each sandwich square with a quail egg. Sprinkle with salt and pepper and serve immediately.

THINK AHEAD
Assemble sandwiches up to 1 day in advance. Cover and refrigerate. Bake just before serving.

COOKS' NOTE
When making the croque madame, use the tip of a small sharp knife to crack open the quail eggs.

The Techniques

A LITTLE EXTRA TIME AND EFFORT

FOR A SPECIAL OCCASION,

FOR FRIENDS, FOR FAMILY –

IT'S WORTH IT.

SHORTCRUST PASTRY

MAKES 300g (10oz)
1⅛ cup (175g) all-purpose flour, sifted
¼ tsp salt
1½ tsp sugar
6 tbsp (90g) chilled butter, cubed
1 egg yolk
2 tbsp water

Place flour, salt, sugar, and butter in a bowl. Also add any flavoring, if using, to the bowl. With 2 knives, cut the butter into the dry ingredients until the mixture resembles fine crumbs (see opposite, left).

Add egg yolk. Mix with a wooden spoon to bring ingredients together. Add remaining water if necessary, ½ tbsp at a time, until the pastry begins to come together (see opposite, right). Bring the pastry together completely with your hands. Turn out of bowl on to a lightly floured surface. Knead briefly to make a smooth round.

THINK AHEAD
Make pastry up to 2 days in advance. Wrap in plastic wrap and refrigerate. Return to room temperature before rolling out. Alternatively, make pastry and freeze up to 1 month in advance. Defrost overnight in refrigerator.

COOKS' NOTE
To guarantee perfect pastry, have all the ingredients very cold. For the best results, place butter and flour in the freezer for 5 minutes before you begin.
As a general rule we do not recommend chilling the pastry, but if the weather is hot or the pastry has been over handled, wrap in plastic wrap and refrigerate for 30 minutes before rolling out.

Cut in the butter with 2 knives.   Add the water ½ tbsp at a time.

FLAVORED SHORTCRUST PASTRY VARIATIONS

Add the specified flavoring to the dry ingredients with the chilled butter. The flavouring ingredient will contribute extra moisture to the pastry, so you may need less liquid than usual to bind the pastry together.

CILANTRO PASTRY
Follow shortcrust pastry recipe, adding 1 tbsp finely chopped cilantro to the dry ingredients.

POPPY SEED PASTRY
Follow shortcrust pastry recipe, adding 1 tsp poppy seeds to the dry ingredients.

ROSEMARY PASTRY
Follow shortcrust pastry recipe, adding 1 tsp finely chopped rosemary to the dry ingredients.

SESAME PASTRY
Follow shortcrust pastry recipe, adding 1 tsp sesame seeds to the dry ingredients.

USING A MACHINE
Follow recipe for shortcrust pastry. Place flour, salt, sugar, and butter, with any flavoring, if using, in a food processor; pulse until mixture resembles fine crumbs. Add egg yolk; pulse until the pastry forms a ball. Add more water as necessary, ½ tbsp at a time. Turn pastry out of the machine on to a lightly floured surface and knead briefly by hand to make a smooth round.

BAKING PASTRY TARTLETS

MAKES 20

1 recipe unbaked shortcrust pastry

ESSENTIAL EQUIPMENT

20 - 1¾in (4.5cm) plain or fluted tartlet pans and 1 - 2in (5cm) plain or fluted pastry cutter

ALTERNATIVELY

2 – 12 cup mini muffin pans and 1 - 2½in (6.5cm) plain or fluted pastry cutter

Baking beans (bought ceramic beans, or alternatively, dried beans)

Preheat oven to 400°F (200°C) .
On a lightly floured surface, roll out pastry to a ⅛in (3mm) thickness. Cut out 20 rounds with the appropriate pastry cutter according to the type of tin specified by the recipe. Use the cut pastry rounds to line the cups(see below, left). Prick the base of each tartlet once with a fork. Refrigerate for 30 minutes before baking.

Fold a piece of baking parchment paper about 12in (30cm) long into small squares about 3in x 3in (7cm x 7cm). Cut the folded paper along the folded ends with scissors. Separate paper to make about 21 paper squares. Do not discard paper liners after using, because they can be used again.

Press a baking parchment paper square into each pastry case. Fill paper with dried beans (see below, right). Bake tartlets until firm, 10 minutes. Remove paper and beans. Continue baking until crisp and golden, 10 minutes.
Cool slightly, then transfer to a wire rack to finish cooling.

THINK AHEAD
Line tartlet pans up to 1 day in advance. Cover and refrigerate. Bake tartlets up to 3 days in advance. Store in an airtight container at room temperature.

COOKS' NOTES
Roll out pastry between 2 large pieces of plastic wrap to prevent pastry from cracking.
Lining the unbaked tartlets with paper and beans helps the pastry keep its shape when baked. If you are an experienced pastry maker and are confident that your pastry won't shrink, place the pastry tartlets in the freezer until solid and bake unlined from frozen.

Line the tartlet pans with the pastry rounds.

Bake tartlets filled with paper and dried beans to prevent pastry from shrinking in the oven.

MAKING STAR-SHAPED TARTLETS

Follow method for rolling out pastry given in the instructions above. Cut out 20 rounds with a 3¼in (8cm) star-shaped pastry cutter. Butter 2 - 12-cup mini muffin pans and line each muffin cup with one star-shaped piece of pastry dough. Follow method for baking pastry (see above).

Cut out the stars.

CHOUX PASTRY

MAKES 500g (1lb)

¾ cup (110g) all-purpose flour, sifted
¾ cup (175ml) water
½ tsp salt
3 tbsp (75g) butter
3 eggs

Place water, salt, and butter in a pan
over a medium heat. Bring just to a
boil and remove from the heat. Add
the flour to the pan, stirring
constantly with a wooden spoon,
until combined (see opposite).
Return the pan to the heat and beat
until the mixture is smooth and pulls
away from the sides of the pan,
1 minute.

Remove from the heat and beat in the
eggs, one at a time, making sure that
each egg is thoroughly incorporated
before adding the next one. Beat
until the mixture is smooth, glossy,
and slightly sticky (see opposite).

USING A MACHINE
We recommend using a food
processor only for making choux
pastry in large quantities (ie;
doubling or tripling the quantities
given above). Make choux pastry as
directed but transfer to a food
processor before adding the eggs.
While the machine is running, add
eggs one at a time until the mixture
is smooth, glossy and slightly sticky.

Add the flour and stir
constantly with a wooden
spoon until combined.

Remove from the heat and
add the eggs one at a time.

CHOUX PUFFS

MAKES 35

1 recipe choux pastry (see page 138)

ESSENTIAL EQUIPMENT

2 tablespoons or a piping bag fitted with a large plain tip

Preheat oven to 350°F (180°C).

Use the tip of the 2 tablespoons to place small walnut-sized spoonfuls of choux pastry, ¾in (2cm) apart, on to a buttered baking sheet (see opposite). Bake until light, crisp and golden, 35 minutes. Cool on a wire rack.

Alternatively, fill the piping bag with the choux pastry (see page 146) and pipe small walnut-sized mounds, ¾in (2cm) apart, on to a buttered baking sheet. Bake until light, crisp and golden, 35 minutes. Cool on a wire rack.

THINK AHEAD
Bake choux puffs up to 3 days in advance. Store in an airtight container at room temperature. Alternatively, freeze baked choux puffs up to 1 month in advance. Defrost overnight in refrigerator. Crisp in a preheated 400°F (200°C) oven for 3 minutes.

COOKS' NOTE
Underbaked puffs do not keep; they turn soggy when filled. It is essential to check one puff for doneness before removing the entire baking sheet from the oven. Split open one puff: the interior must be hollow and completely dry. Continue baking if necessary until the puffs are completely dry.

Use the tip of 2 tablespoons to shape puffs.

Alternatively, use a piping bag.

CHOUX MINI ECLAIRS

MAKES 30

1 recipe choux pastry (see page 138)

ESSENTIAL EQUIPMENT

piping bag fitted with a large plain tip

Preheat oven to 350°F (180°C). Fill a piping bag with choux pastry (see page 146). Pipe out 30 spiral shaped strips about 2in (5cm) long on to a buttered baking sheet. Leave 4cm (1½in) between each strip to allow for expansion in the oven. Bake until light, crisp and golden, 35 minutes. Cool on a wire rack.

BREAD DOUGH

MAKES ¾ lb (400g)

1⅔ CUPS (250g) bread flour

¼ tsp salt

⅝ cup (165ml) tepid water

1 tsp olive oil

1 tsp dried yeast

Place the flour in a bowl and make a well in the center. Place the salt along the raised edge of the flour. Pour the water with the oil into the well. Sprinkle the yeast over the liquid. Let stand for 5 minutes; stir to dissolve. Draw in the flour from the sides of the bowl with a spoon (see opposite, top), and mix to make a rough, sticky dough.

Turn out dough on to a lightly floured surface. Use the heel of one hand to gently push the dough away from you. At the same time, use your other hand to rotate the dough slightly towards you, guiding it around in a circle (see opposite, middle). Repeat these kneading actions until the dough is smooth, shiny, and elastic, 10 minutes.

Put the dough in a clean bowl and cover with a dish towel (see opposite, bottom). Let it rise until doubled in size, about 1½ hours. Deflate the dough by pressing down with the palm of your hand. The dough is now ready to be shaped.

THINK AHEAD

Make and knead 12 hours in advance. Cover and let it rise in refrigerator overnight. Let stand at room temperature for 30 minutes before shaping. Shape and bake according to the recipe.

COOKS' NOTE

The quantity of liquid required will often vary according to the type of flour used, as well as the level of humidity and temperature on the day of breadmaking. It is best to err on the side of making a dough too soft rather than too dry. Add extra water after drawing in the flour to form dough, as necessary, 1 tbsp at a time.

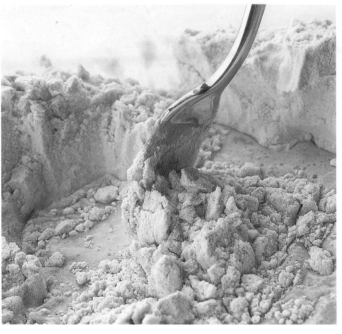

Draw in the flour from the sides of the bowl.

Knead the dough until smooth and elastic.

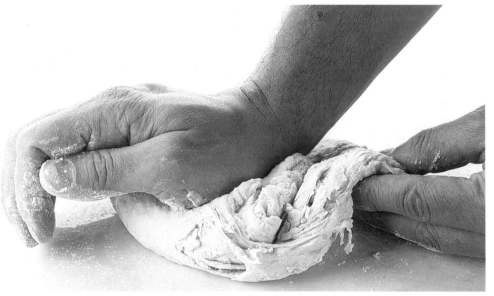

USING A MACHINE

Follow recipe and method for bread dough, but place ingredients, after they have been mixed to a rough dough, into the bowl of a heavy-duty mixer fitted with a dough hook. To knead, set the mixer at low speed for 10 minutes. Alternatively, use the bowl of a food processor fitted with a plastic dough blade. To knead, use the pulse button for 30 seconds at a time, until dough is smooth and elastic, 4 minutes.

Cover the dough with a tea towel to rise.

VANILLA MERINGUE

MAKES ⅔ lb (300ml)

2 egg whites at room temperature
½ cup (125g) sugar
½ tsp vanilla extract

Put the egg whites in a large, clean bowl and whisk until the meringue holds soft peaks (see opposite).

Add the sugar, 1 tbsp at a time, whisking well after each addition (see opposite). Continue whisking until the whites are stiff and glossy. With a rubber spatula, fold in vanilla, and additional flavoring, if using, according to the instructions given for the flavor variations (see below).

COOKS' NOTE
Make sure the bowl is completely grease-free or the whites will not stiffen. If in doubt, wipe with paper towel dipped in vinegar and dry the bowl before you begin.

A daring, but effective, way to check if the whites are sufficiently stiff is to hold the bowl upside down: the meringue should not fall out!

FLAVORED MERINGUE VARIATIONS
Add the flavoring to the meringue with the vanilla. Fold in with a spatula until evenly combined.

CHOCOLATE MERINGUE
Fold in 1 tsp sifted cocoa powder with the vanilla.

HAZELNUT MERINGUE
Fold in 2 tbsp ground blanched hazelnuts with the vanilla.

MUSCAVADO MERINGUE
Fold in 1 tbsp dark brown sugar with the vanilla.

PISTACHIO MERINGUE
Fold in 1 tbsp chopped unsalted pistachios with the vanilla.

Whisk egg whites to soft peaks.   Add sugar 1 tbsp at a time.

VANILLA MERINGUE KISSES

MAKES 40

1 recipe unbaked vanilla meringue (see opposite, left)

ESSENTIAL EQUIPMENT
piping bag fitted with large star nozzle

Preheat oven to 250°F (120°C). Fill piping bag with meringue (see page 146). Pipe 40 meringue rosettes, 1in (2.5cm) apart, onto baking parchment-lined baking sheets. Bake until crisp and dry, 1 hour. Cool completely before removing from the baking sheet.

THINK AHEAD
Bake up to 1 week in advance. Store in an airtight container at room temperature.

Pipe kisses 2.5cm (1in) apart.

MINI MERINGUES

MAKES 20

1 recipe unbaked vanilla meringue (see opposite, left)

Preheat oven to 350°F (180°C) . Use the tip of two teaspoons to place small walnut-sized spoonfuls of meringue, 1in (2.5cm) apart, on to baking parchment-lined baking sheets. Make an indention in the center of each mini meringue with the back of one teaspoon. Bake for 5 minutes; then turn the oven temperature down to 250°F (120°C). Continue baking until firm to the touch, 20 minutes. Cool completely before removing the mini meringues from the baking sheet.

THINK AHEAD
Bake up to 2 days in advance.
Store in an airtight container at room temperature.

Shape meringue with the back of a teaspoon.

MAYONNAISE

MAKES 1¼ cups (300ml)

2 egg yolks
1 tsp dijon mustard
1 tbsp red wine vinegar
½ tsp salt
pinch black pepper
1 tsp sugar
1¼ cups (300ml) sunflower oil
black pepper

ESSENTIAL EQUIPMENT
wire whisk

Make sure that all the ingredients are at room temperature before you begin. Set a deep bowl on a cloth to prevent it from slipping as you whisk. Whisk the egg yolks, mustard, vinegar, salt, pepper, and sugar together in a bowl until thick and creamy, 1 minute (see opposite, left).

Place the oil in a measuring cup. Whisk in the oil a drop at a time until the mixture thickens. Add the remaining oil in a thin, steady stream, whisking constantly until thick and glossy (see opposite, right). Whisk in any flavoring, if using, according to the recipe variations. Adjust seasoning, adding more mustard, vinegar, salt, pepper or sugar to taste.

THINK AHEAD
Make mayonnaise up to 3 days in advance. Cover and refrigerate. Return to room temperature before stirring to prevent the mayonnaise from separating.

COOKS' NOTE
If the ingredients are too cold or the oil is added too quickly, the mayonnaise may separate. Don't throw it away! Combine 1 tsp vinegar and 1 tsp creamy mustard in a clean bowl. Whisk in the separated mayonnaise drop by drop until the mixture re-emulsifies.

SAFETY WARNING ON RAW EGGS
Because of the potential risk of salmonella, pregnant women, young children and anyone with a weakened immune system should avoid eating raw eggs. Make sure you use only the freshest (preferably organic) eggs, and, if in doubt, substitute ready-made mayonnaise (see opposite).

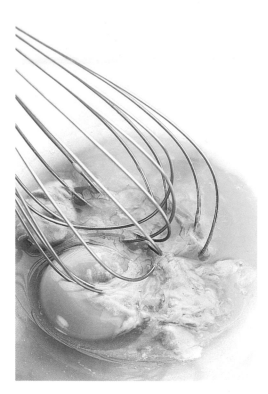

Whisk the yolks until thick and creamy.

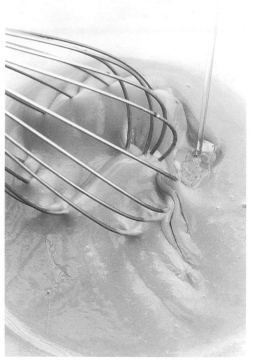

Add the oil in a steady stream.

FLAVORED MAYONNAISE VARIATIONS
Whisk flavoring into the finished mayonnaise. Make sure that the flavoring and mayonnaise are at room temperature before you begin.

LEMON MAYONNAISE
Whisk 1 tbsp lemon juice into 1 recipe mayonnaise.

LEMON AIOLI
Crush 2 garlic cloves. Whisk crushed garlic into 1 recipe lemon mayonnaise (see variation above).

LIGHT LEMON MAYONNAISE
Whisk 2 tbsp warm water into 1 recipe lemon mayonnaise (see above) to lighten flavor, color, and consistency.

USING READY-MADE MAYONNAISE
Use ready made mayonnaise when in need of a time saving short-cut or if health concerns are an issue for you. Seek out a good quality whole egg brand of mayonnaise and enhance the flavor by whisking in dijon mustard, sugar, and red wine vinegar or lemon juice to taste.

USING A MACHINE
Follow recipe for mayonnaise. Place the egg yolks, mustard, vinegar, salt, pepper, and sugar with 3 tbsp of the oil in a blender or food processor; process until blended, 10 seconds. While the machine is running, pour in the remaining oil in a thin, steady stream, until the mixture emulsifies and becomes thick and glossy. Pulse in any flavoring, if using. Adjust seasoning, adding more mustard, vinegar, salt, pepper or sugar to taste.

COOKS' NOTE
If using a food processor, depending on its capacity, you may need to stop the machine at intervals to scrape down the sides and over the bottom of the bowl with a spatula.

LEMON HOLLANDAISE

MAKES ¾ cup (175ml)
½ cup (125g) butter
2 tbsp water
2 egg yolks
salt and white pepper
juice of ½ lemon

Melt the butter; then skim the foam from the surface with a spoon. Let it to cool until tepid. Place a heatproof bowl over a pan of simmering water set on a low heat. Make sure the bottom of the bowl is not in direct contact with the hot water. Place water and yolks with a pinch each salt and pepper in the bowl. Whisk the ingredients to a light and frothy mixture that holds the trail of the whisk, 3 minutes (see opposite, left). Remove the pan from the heat.

Whisk in butter, a little at a time, vigorously whisking after each addition, until the mixture emulsifies and becomes thick and creamy (see opposite, right). Gradually whisk in the lemon juice. Adjust seasoning, adding more salt, pepper or lemon juice to taste.

THINK AHEAD
Make hollandaise up to 30 minutes in advance. Keep warm in a bowl over a pan of hot water placed off the heat. Alternatively, make hollandaise up to 2 days in advance. Cover and refrigerate. Place in a heatproof bowl over a pan of simmering water set over a low heat. Make sure the base of the bowl is not in direct contact with the water. Warm through, whisking occasionally, until tepid, 10 minutes.

COOKS' NOTE
If the butter is added too quickly, the hollandaise may separate. Don't throw it away! Combine 1 tbsp water and 1 egg yolk in a clean bowl over a pan of simmering water set on a low heat. Make sure the base of the bowl is not in contact with the water. Whisk to a light and frothy mixture that holds that trail of the whisk, 3 minutes. Remove the pan from the heat. Whisk in the separated

Whisk the water and egg yolks to a light, frothy mixture.

Add the butter a little at a time.

SAUCE BEARNAISE

Place 3 tbsp red wine vinegar, 6 peppercorns, 1 finely chopped shallot, and 1 sprig each tarragon and chervil in a small pan. Bring the ingredients to a boil over medium heat and continue cooking until the liquid is reduced to 1 tbsp. Cool and strain. Now follow the recipe for hollandaise, omitting the lemon juice. Place the reduction in a bowl with the water, egg yolks, salt, and pepper and follow the recipe method. Stir in 1 tsp each of finely chopped tarragon and chervil after the butter has been added. Adjust seasoning, adding more salt and pepper to taste.

USING A MACHINE

Follow recipe for lemon hollandaise. Place egg yolks, salt and pepper in a food processor or blender. Bring butter, water and lemon juice to simmering point in a small pan. While the machine is running, pour in the hot butter mixture in a slow, steady stream until the mixture emulsifies and becomes thick and creamy. Adjust seasoning, adding more salt, pepper, or lemon juice to taste.

COOKS' NOTE
If using a food processor, depending on its capacity, you may need to stop the machine at intervals to scrape down the sides and over the bottom of the bowl with a spatula.

VANILLA PASTRY CREAM

MAKES ¾ cup (175ml)

2 eggs

2 tbsp sugar

2 tsp flour

½ cup(125ml) milk

¼ tsp vanilla extract

Place the eggs and sugar in a bowl. Whisk until thick and light, 2 minutes. Add the flour and continue whisking until smooth (see opposite, top left).

In a small heavy-bottomed saucepan, bring the milk just to a boil over a medium heat. Pour the boiling milk into the egg mixture, while whisking constantly until the mixture is completely smooth (see opposite, top right). Pour the mixture through a strainer into a pan and place over a medium heat.

Cook the strained pastry cream until very thick, stirring constantly, 2 minutes (see opposite, middle left). Reduce heat to low and cook, stirring constantly until pastry cream no longer tastes of raw flour, 2 minutes. Stir in vanilla with additional flavoring, if using, according to the recipe variation (see page 145).

Transfer pastry cream to a bowl to cool. Press waxed paper directly onto the surface of the pastry cream to stop a skin from forming (see opposite, middle right).

THINK AHEAD
Make pastry cream up to 2 days in advance. Cover and refrigerate.

COOKS' NOTE
Don't worry if lumps form as the pastry cream cooks; continue cooking. After removing from the heat simply push the cooked pastry cream through a strainer to eliminate any lumps. Be sure to allow the pastry cream to cool completely before chilling. If it is not completely cold when refrigerated, the steam will condense and form watery puddles on the surface of the cream.

Add the flour and whisk until smooth.

Whisk constantly while adding the milk to the egg.

Cook the pastry cream until very thick.

Cover with waxed paper to cool.

WHIPPING CREAM

For whipping, cream must contain a minimum of 30% butterfat.

Make sure the cream, bowl, and whisk are well chilled before whipping: place in the refrigerator for 30 minutes or in the freezer for 10 minutes before you begin. Pour the cream into a bowl and whisk until it starts to thicken. Continue whisking until the cream is light and just holds a soft peak when the whisk is lifted. If the recipe requires stiff peaks, continue whisking until the cream stands up when the whisk is removed, about 1 minute more.

Whisk cream until it holds soft peaks. Add sugar and continue whisking until the cream re-stiffens to soft or stiff peaks, 1 -2 minutes.

THINK AHEAD
Make whipped cream up to 4 hours in advance. Cover and refrigerate.

COOKS' NOTE
If your cream begins to look granular and yellowish as you are whisking you have over whipped it. To remedy, gently fold in a little extra cream, 1 tbsp at a time, to bring it back to a smooth, silky texture.

Whisk until cream holds soft peaks.

Add sugar to whipped cream and whisk to re-stiffen.

FLAVORED PASTRY CREAM VARIATION

CHOCOLATE PASTRY CREAM

Follow the recipe and method for vanilla pastry cream. Melt 3½ oz (100g) bittersweet chocolate (see opposite). Stir melted chocolate into the pastry cream with the vanilla until thoroughly combined and smooth in texture.

MAKING CARAMEL

Place sugar and water in a heavy-bottomed pan over a low heat. Stir constantly with a wooden spoon. Completely dissolve the sugar before allowing the liquid to come to a boil. Raise the heat to medium and bring the syrup to a boil. Do not stir the syrup. Boil rapidly until the syrup starts to brown around the edge of the pan. Lower the heat and continue cooking, swirling the pan once or twice so that the caramel colors evenly. Remove the pan from the heat shortly before the caramel reaches the desired color, since it will continue to cook from the heat of the pan.

COOKS' NOTE
Once the syrup has boiled, do not stir because doing so might cause crystallization. If your caramel is coloring too fast, stop it cooking by plunging the bottom of the pan in to a bowl of cold water. If it sets too hard, warm it gently through in the pan over a low heat until it melts, taking care not to let it boil or to continue to cook further.

MELTING CHOCOLATE

Chocolate should be melted gently and slowly as it will scorch if overheated.

Break chocolate into small pieces. Place in a heatproof bowl over a pan of hot, not simmering, water set over a very low heat. Make sure the bottom of the bowl is not in contact with the water. Once the chocolate starts to melt, stir frequently. When about half the chocolate has melted, remove the pan from the heat and stir constantly until smooth, glossy, and completely melted.

COOKS' NOTE
Make sure the bowl fits snugly over the pan. If any steam escapes from the simmering water below and falls on to the chocolate as it melts, the chocolate may suddenly become rough, stiff, and lumpy. If this happens, remove the chocolate from the heat immediately and stir in sunflower oil, 1 tsp at a time, until the chocolate becomes smooth again.

Light caramel is pale gold in color and is used for coating pastries.

Dark caramel is dark golden brown in color and is used for lining moulds.

Once the chocolate begins to melt, remove from the heat and stir constantly until completely melted.

PREPARE THE PIPING BAG
Make sure the tip is fitted securely, then twist the bag above the tip to prevent leakage while filling.

FILL THE BAG
Fold the top of the bag over your hand to form a collar; spoon in the filling.

TWIST THE BAG TO PIPE
Twist the top of the bag, until the filling is visible in the tip, to clear any air pockets before you begin.

MAKING A PAPER
PIPING BAG

Fold a 9½in (25cm) square of baking parchment in half diagonally and cut along the fold (see above). Bring one point of the triangle to the center to form a cone (see top right).

Wrap the remaining point of the triangle around to meet the other two points. Pull all 3 points tightly together to create a sharp point and fold flap inside (see bottom right). Crease the flap to hold the shape of the cone together.

PIPING, TOPPING OR
FILLING

Hold the piping bag in a vertical position and exert pressure on the bag with the fingers and palm of one hand to force out the filling. Guide the tip with the other hand. Exert a small amount of pressure on the bag to make a small rosette for topping.

Apply more pressure to make a large rosette for filling. Lift up the tip quickly to finish the rosette.

CUTTING INTO JULIENNE STRIPS

Cut vegetable into very thin slices, about ⅛ in (0.3cm) thick. Cut the stacked slices into thin even-sized strips the size of matchsticks. To save time, stack the slices a few at a time before cutting into strips.

PEELING TOMATOES

Cut a small cross, on the bottom of each tomato. Drop tomatoes into boiling water. Remove when you see the edges of the each cross begin to loosen, 10-20 seconds, depending on the ripeness. Drain, then immerse in cold water. Peel off the loosened skins, using the tip of a knife.

SEEDING TOMATOES

Cut tomatoes into quarters. With a sharp knife, cut out seeds and core.

Seeding tomatoes is crucial in many recipes because the seeds exude juice and may make fresh salsas and garnishes watery.

CUTTING INTO FINE DICE

Cut the vegetable into thin, even slices. Stack the slices a few at a time. Cut the stack lengthwise to make equal-sized strips. Cut across to make an even-sized dice.

BROILING AND PEELING PEPPERS

Roast pepper quarters skin side up under a hot broiler until charred and wrinkled, 5-10 minutes. Place in a plastic bag or a bowl with a plate on top and let them cool. The steam released by the peppers as they cool will loosen the skin.
Uncover cooled peppers. Peel off the charred skin, using the tip of a small knife. Scrape rather than rinse off any remaining bits of skin. Rinsing the pepper will wash away the roasted flavor.

PEELING CITRUS FRUIT

Cut a thick slice from both ends to expose the flesh. Stand upright and cut away peel and white pith, following the curve of the fruit.

SEGMENTING CITRUS FRUIT

Hold peeled fruit in one hand. Use the tip of the knife to cut down both sides of one white membrane to release each segment.

MAKING HERB SPRIGS

Select only the freshest, greenest leaves when making herbs sprigs for garnishing. Strip the leaves from the stalks and divide any larger sprigs into smaller pieces.

MAKING EDIBLE SKEWERS

Use edible skewers to add extra flavor to skewered foods. Some ideas used in the recipe section are illustrated here. Bay and thyme stalks are not shown, but also make effective skewers when their stems are stiff and thick enough to hold food.

LEMON GRASS SKEWERS

Remove and discard the tough outer skin from the lemon grass stalks. Cut in half lengthwise, keeping the stalks attached by the root. Cut into 4in (10cm) lengths to use for skewers.

ASSEMBLING A WRAP

ROLLING UP THE FILLING

Place the wrap base on a piece of plastic wrap and cover with the filling. Use the plastic wrap underneath to help you as you carefully roll up the base around the filling as tightly as possible.

SUGARCANE STICKS

If using fresh sugarcane, peel with a vegetable peeler and trim to 4in (10cm) lengths. Cut each sugarcane piece length-wise into ¼in (0.5cm) thick slices. Cut slices into ¼in (0.5cm) strips.

ROSEMARY SKEWERS

Strip the leaves from the stalks. Leave just a few leaves at one end. Sharpen the other end with a sharp knife to make threading food onto the skewer easier.

SECURING THE ROLL

Twist each end of plastic wrap tightly to secure and shape the roll.

MAKING PARMESAN SHAVINGS

MAKING AN INDENTION

Cut out a slightly curved indention from the longest side of the piece of chese with a sharp knife.

SHAVING THE PARMESAN

Use a vegetable peeler to shave curls from the indention.

COVERING AIRTIGHT

Always press plastic wrap against the surface of foods to keep out as much air as possible. The oxygen in the air increases the spoilage and discoloration of many foods, such as avocado. Protecting food from the oxidising properties of air will keep food looking and tasting fresher longer.

FREEZING UNBAKED ITEMS

To freeze unbaked items, spread out on a baking sheet and place in freezer uncovered until hard, 30 minutes. Once the items are frozen, pack into plastic freezer bags or an airtight container and return to the freezer. Remember to label items clearly for easier retrieval.

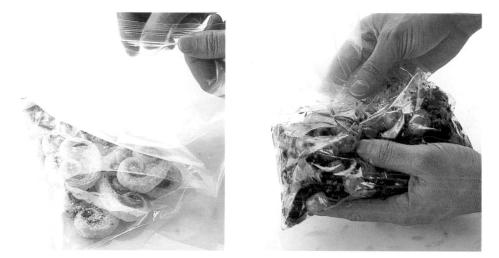

SEALING AIRTIGHT

Before sealing, expel all the air to make storage bags airtight. Zip lock plastic bags are ideal for storing both wet and dry foods. Zip lock bags are also useful for marinating. They allow the marinade to be evenly distributed around the ingredients.

HOT WEATHER COOKING

When planning a menu for hot weather, choose recipes that are fresh, light, and simple to prepare. Not only do rich, creamy foods require cool temperatures for storage if made ahead, but they tend to be less popular in the warmer months. We advise starting as early in the day as possible, when the temperature is coolest. Do not attempt too many jobs at a time. Get one recipe finished and place immediately in a storage container, in the refrigerator, or in another cool place. Coolers with ice packs are extremely useful in hot weather. They provide additional and portable refrigeration, especially when entertaining away from the house.

Be careful to keep all food out of direct sunlight, both when storing and serving. For outdoor entertaining, find a shady, sheltered spot - and make sure it will still be in the shade during the hours you plan to entertain.

STORING IN LAYERS

Cooked pancakes, fritters, and raw pastries and doughs are moist and may stick together if packed too tightly. Store in single layers in an airtight container with waxed paper or paper towelsplaced in between the layers to keep items separated.

THE PARTY

PLAN AHEAD,
CHOOSE A MENU WITH VARIETY, AND
PRESENT WITH SIMPLICITY AND STYLE;
YOU ARE SET FOR SUCCESS.

THE PLAN

THE MENU

The most crucial part of good menu composition is to include a variety of tastes, textures, aromas, and colors. Try to create a menu with contrasts. Choose a variety of canapés that will give your guests a balance of sweet, sharp, spicy, salty, and sour flavors. Remember that canapés should always be a small bite with a big flavor. Here are a few things to consider when planning your menu.

• Never attempt a menu with all brand new recipes. Experiment with unfamiliar recipes before the day of the party. Be sure to mix in a few tried and tested favorites.

• Let the seasons be your inspiration. Seasonal ingredients will be reasonably priced, widely available, and at their flavorful best. This will also help you avoid a time-wasting search for one ingredient.

• Review the guest list for vegetarians and anyone with special diet requirements, whether religious or medical.

• Provide something to please everybody. Be sure to consider both the more and the less adventurous guests. Include some old fashioned canapé classics as well as some creative new ones.

• Take into account how ingredients are prepared, whether broiled, fried, baked, roasted, or raw, and try and achieve a good balance.

• Aim for a varied mix of ingredients and try not to repeat the same ingredient more than once in a menu.

• Include at least 2 hot canapés for parties during the colder months of the year.

THE QUANTITIES

A range of different factors play a part in how much your guests will eat. Hors d'oeuvres consumption goes up and down in direct relation to when, where, and who.

TIME OF YEAR: we are heartier eaters in the colder months.

TIME OF DAY: consider when your guests will have last eaten a full meal. Guests who have had to travel or have arrived straight from the office to a party will eat more.

LOCATION: a crowded space makes serving difficult and, as a result, reduces the quantities consumed.

GUESTS: friends and family will not be afraid to eat heartily at a causal gathering. At a formal occasion, where everyone is more reserved, they tend to eat less. At charity events, where the guests have paid for their invitations, people will expect there to be more food served.

Use the following guidelines to help determine quantities of hors d'oeuvres in menu planning.

Our basic rule is to allow 6 pieces per guest for the first hour and 4 pieces for each additional hour that the party continues.

Focus on doing less better.
We prefer to offer a smaller variety of hors d'oeuvres, but each in greater quantities. You'll have time to make a superior recipe and save on time and cost. We recommend serving 10 hors d'oeuvres per guest by choosing 5 different recipes and doubling the quantities.

For **pre-lunch or dinner drinks**, allow 3 pieces per guest and choose 3 different hors d'oeuvres.

For **hors d'oeuvres served instead of a first course before a lunch or dinner party**, allow 5 pieces per guest and choose 5 different hors d'oeuvres.

For a **2-3 hour cocktail party**, allow approximately 10 pieces per guest and choose either 5 or 10 different hors d'oeuvres.

For a **hors d'oeuvres only party served in place of a meal**, allow 14 pieces per guest and choose either 7 or 14 different kinds.

For a **stand-up wedding reception,** allow 12 pieces per guest and choose 8 to 10 different savory hors d'oeuvres and 2 to 4 different sweet hors d'oeuvres.

THE STRATEGY

Parties are to enjoy - and that goes for you as well as your guests. A party at home is more relaxed when you are well organized. Planning is everything.

• Make two shopping lists, one for non-perishable ingredients that can be purchased in advance and another for foods that must be bought fresh the day before the party.

• Think through each recipe and make a cooking timetable. List all the stages of preparation, from complete recipes suitable for freezing to any last minute garnishing that needs to be done just before serving.

• Prepare ingredients and cook ahead as much as possible so you have plenty of time to complete the final preparations without suffering from party day panic. Use the THINK AHEAD advice provided for each recipe in the book.

• Enlist family and friends or hire professionals to help you serve.

• Take stock of your serving dishes several days before the party. Make sure you have enough and make arrangements to buy, borrow, or hire if necessary.

THE PRESENTATION

GENERAL RULES

Hors D'Oeuvres must be tempting to the eye as well as pleasing to the palate. If food looks fabulous, people will feel confident that it tastes fabulous too. Follow these tips for beautiful, mouthwatering results.

• Arrange one, or at most two, kinds of hors d'oeuvres on a serving tray at a time. Presenting too many kinds is not only visually confusing, but unpractical, causing guests to break the flow of conversation to make their choice.

• Place hors d'oeuvres in neat, evenly-spaced rows to maximize their aesthetic appeal.

• Odd numbers look better than even numbers, and diagonal lines are more pleasing to the eye than straight ones. Remember these golden rules of food presentation when arranging hors d'oeuvres on a serving tray.

• Don't overcrowd the serving trays. A densely packed arrangement can look cluttered and messy rather than generous.

• Keep garnishes simple. Over decorated food can look fussy and unappetizing.

• Make sure your guests have somewhere to put skewers or shells after they have finished eating an hors d'oeuvre.

• Avoid plates and platters that will be heavy or difficult to pass.

• Get help assembling hors d'oeuvres and arranging garnishes and trays. These final preparations are great fun when shared with family and friends.

• Have more napkins on hand than you think you will need. When offering food, always have cocktail napkins handy for any guests who might need one.

NATURAL CONTAINERS AND GARNISHES

Fresh, edible garnishes are a simple, natural way to decorate (see pages 156-157).

Use brightly colored fruits and vegetables to garnish platters and trays. Hollow them out to make edible containers for nibbles, dippers, and dips. A serrated knife and a melon ball cutter (see page 14) are essential tools for this. Prepare edible decorations up to 1 day in advance and store covered with damp paper towels in an airtight container in the refrigerator.

CREATIVE SERVING IDEAS

Innovative presentation need not be expensive and always makes food memorable and for some, even more delicious (see pages 158-159).

Fresh herbs make natural sticks for skewering (see page 148), fragrant bouquets for garnishing, and an attractive lining for a serving tray. Choose herbs unlikely to wilt, like rosemary, thyme, oregano, bay, lemon grass, and sage.

Use leaves to line trays or platters. Be sure to wipe fresh leaves clean with a damp cloth. Banana, fig, vine, palm, and cabbages leaves of various colors are ideal. Dried leaves, such as chestnut or lotus, should be brushed with sunflower oil before using.

Visit Asian and other ethnic markets for unusual but inexpensive serving ideas. For example, use a bamboo steamer as a serving dish, chopsticks as skewers, sushi mats a noodles to line trays. These are all easy and inexpensive ways to add style to the presentation of an Asian-themed hors d'oeuvre menu. Use your imagination to come up with other themes.

STATIONARY HORS D'OEUVRES

Hors D'Oeuvre parties are an easy way to entertain a large number of people at home. Think: no chairs, no plates, no cutlery! If you are expecting more than 15 guests, you will need helping hands, either hired professionals or recruits from family and friends. But not all the food has to be passed around on trays. A less formal approach is to arrange everything on stationary platters, trays, bowls, and baskets on tables around the room and allow people to serve themselves.

NATURAL CONTAINERS AND GARNISHES

1 MINIATURE PINEAPPLES: Use whole to decorate a stationary arrangement of canapés.

2 NAVEL ORANGE: Julienne peel to garnish sweet or savory canapés.

3 SWEET RED PEPPER: Hollow out to hold dips and sauces.

4 SMALL AUBERGINE: Use whole to decorate a serving tray.

5 BUTTERNUT SQUASH: Hollow out to hold vegetable dippers.

6 ITALIAN PEPPER: Use whole to decorate a serving tray of spicy canapés.

7 STAR FRUIT: Slice to garnish a serving tray of sweet canapés.

8 CHARENTAIS MELON: Hollow out to hold fruit skewers and dipping sauces.

9 PURPLE AND WHITE CABBAGE: Hollow out to use as a container for dips.

10 LIMES AND LEMONS: Peel and segment to garnish individual canapés.

CREATIVE SERVING IDEAS

1. **WICKER BASKET:** To serve stacked canapés (see page 132).

2. **SUSHI MATT:** To line a serving tray (see page 90).

3. **BANANA LEAVES:** To line a serving tray (see page 73).

4. **COARSE SEA SALT:** To support shellfish canapés (see page 104).

5. **BAMBOO STEAMER:** To serve Asian-style canapés.

6. **CHOP STICKS:** As an alternative to wooden skewers (see page 71).

7. **SOBA NOODLES:** To line a serving tray (see page 94).

8. **LEMON GRASS STALKS:** To skewer grilled chicken (see page 74).

9. **WOODEN TOOTHPICKS:** To skewer bite-sized canapés (see page 68).

10. **WOODEN SKEWERS**

11. **WOVEN TABLE MAT**

12. **SLATTED WOODEN TRAY**

13. **ROSEMARY SPRIG SKEWERS** (see page 71).

MENU SUGGESTIONS

(see the index for page numbers)

DO NOTHING ON THE DAY

Consult this list for hors d'oeuvres that keep you out of the kitchen on the day of the party. All of them can be made at least 1 day ahead and transferred from storage container to serving tray with minimal effort.

Parmesan and Anchovy Palmiers

Cherry and Almond Frangipane Tartlets

Chorizo Puffs

Citrus Ginger Cream Tartlets

Creamy Blue Cheese and Spring Onion Dip

Crispy Potato Skins

Crunchy Sweet and Spicy Pecans

Curry Puffs

Curry Spiced Yogurt, Cilantro, and Mango Chutney Dip

Ham and Dijon Mini Croissants

Egg, Caper, and Cress Finger Sandwiches

Herbed Yogurt Dip

Herbed Pita Crisps

Honey Mustard and Prosciutto Palmiers

Mediterranean Marinated Olives

Mini Gougères

Olive Cheese Balls

Oven-Dried Root and Fruit Chips

Rare Roast Beef and Horseradish Mayonnaise Finger Sandwiches

Roasted Red Pepper, Feta, and Mint Dip

Rolled Smoked Ham Crepes with Tarragon and Mustard Cream

Rolled Ricotta and Sage Crepes with Parmesan Shavings

Salsa Romesco Dip

Savory Sables

Smoked Salmon and Chive Cream Finger Sandwiches

Smoked Salmon Ruggelash

Smoked Salmon Sushi Rice Balls

Spicy Peanut Dip

Spinach, Smoked Trout, and Herbed Cream Roulades

Spiced Party Nuts

Spiced Roasted Eggplant Dip

Sun-dried Tomato and Cannellini Bean Dip

Sun-dried Tomato Pesto Palmiers

Swiss Cheese Allumettes

Texas Red Bean Wraps with Cilantro Crema

Vegetable Dippers

HORS D'OEUVRES FROM THE GRILL

Let your guests mingle over some tasty nibbles while the barbecue heats up. Follow with food hot off the grill. Finish with a decadent dessert.

Crunchy Sweet and Spicy Pecans

Herbed Yogurt Dip with Crispy Potato Skins

Clams with Ginger and Lime Butter

Ginger Hoisin Mini Chicken Drumsticks

Lemon Chili Shrimp Sticks

Curried Coconut Chicken Sticks

Quesadilla Triangles with Hot Pepper Relish

Strawberry and Pistachio Mini Meringues

LIGHT BITES FOR AL FRESCO ENTERTAINING

A midsummer menu for a lively party under the hot midday sun - serve in place of a first course, or double up the quantities and make it a meal.

Chilled Spiced Chickpea Soup with Avocado Salsa

Tomato and Basil Crostini

Basil Marinated Mozzarella and Cherry Tomato Skewers

Radish Cups with Black Olive Tapenade

Mini Peking Duck Pancakes with Plum Sauce

CELEBRATION BRUNCH FOR THE FAMILY

Classic hors d'oeuvres for a brunch party appeal to young and old alike. Perfect with your favorite fruit juice and fizz, everything but the croque monsieur can be prepared a day ahead and assembled in advance.

Ham and Dijon Mini Croissants

Egg and Bacon Puffs

Mini Croque Monsieur

Baby Bagels with Cream Cheese, Lox, and Dill

Rosemary Mini Muffins with Smoked Ham and Peach Relish

Tiny Dill Scones with Smoked Trout and Horseradish Cream

Tropical Fruit Brochettes with Passion Fruit and Mascarpone Dip

ELEGANT APPETIZERS FOR A SHORT FORMAL RECEPTION

Prelude to an elegant evening of entertaining - many of these can be started ahead, but you will need an extra pair of hands just before serving to help with the final touches.

Chive-Tied Crepe Bundles with Smoked Salmon and Lemon Creme Fraiche

Tarragon and Mustard Lobster Bouchees

Baby Baked Potatoes with Sour Cream and Caviar

Asparagus Croutes with Lemon Hollandaise

Carpaccio Canapés

FAST AND FABULOUS MENU

Good food in a hurry - use the THINK AHEAD notes to get the dip and crostini finished before guests arrive. Grill the chicken and shrimp sticks to order. You've done it!

Creamy Blue Cheese and Scallion Dip with Herbed Pita Crisps

Avocado and Goat Cheese Crostini

Curried Coconut Chicken Sticks

Tangy Thai Shrimp Skewers

PORTABLE HORS D'OEUVRES FOR AN EVENING PICNIC

A varied menu that can be completely prepared in advance and transported easily - bring along wicker baskets, wooden bowls, and large napkins, and arrange the food when you arrive at the perfect spot.

Swiss Cheese Allumettes

Salsa Romesco Dip with
  Vegetable Dippers

Mini Pissaladiere

Spicy Pork Empanaditas with Chunky
  Avocado Relish

Roasted Red Onion and Thyme
  Foccacine

Minted Feta and Pine Nut Filo Rolls
  with Lemon Aioli

Triple Chocolate Biscottini with
  Hazelnuts

•

CANDELIGHT WINTER WEDDING AT HOME

A welcoming, warming menu of traditional hors d'oeuvres with a twist - we recommend starting the preparation two days in advance; refer to the THINK AHEAD *notes.*

Carrot, Honey, and Ginger Soup Cups

Cocktail Salmon and Dill Cakes with
  Crème Fraîche Tartare

Field Mushroom and Hollandaise
  Tartlets

Orange Muffins with Smoked Turkey
  and Cranberry Sauce

Filo Tartlets with Smoked Salmon,
  Cracked Pepper and Lime

Quail Egg, Caviar, and Chervil
  Croustades

Grilled Beef Fillet with Salsa
  Verde Croutes

Chive Pancakes with Crème Fraîche
  and Red Onion Confit

Cherubs on Horseback

Mini Mango Galettes

Bitter Chocolate Tartlets

Mini Sticky Orange and
  Almond Cakes

MEDITERRANEAN FEAST

A big on flavor, make ahead menu for a special occasion.

Parmesan and Pine Nut Biscottini
  with Green Olives

Sundried Tomato and Cannellini Bean
  Dip with Herbed Pita Crisps

Spicy Shrimp Crostini

Artichoke and Gorgonzola Focaccine

Feta, Olive, and Rosemary Quichettes

Polenta Crostini with Tomato and
  Black Olive Salsa

Chicken, Prosciutto, and Sage
  Spiedini with Roasted Pepper Aioli

•

TEMPTING TREATS FOR AN INFORMAL EVENING WITH FRIENDS

Simple and delicious food for a relaxing and enjoyable evening - everything can be made before your guests arrive. The skewers are the only last minute item needing attention.

Mediterranean Marinated Olives

Savory Sables

Roasted Red Pepper, Feta, and Mint
  Dip with Vegetable Dippers

Filo Tartlets with Spicy
  Cilantro Shrimp

Wild Rice and Scallion Pancakes
  with Avocado Lime Salsa

Sesame Soy Glazed Beef Skewers

Mini Chocolate Truffle Cake

•

VEGETARIAN HORS D'OEUVRES FOR A CROWD

Fabulous finger foods without meat or fish - combine a range of vegetables with fragrant herbs, pungent cheeses, and crisp pastries to tempt even the most hardened of carnivores.

Olive Cheese Balls

Twisted Parsley Breadsticks

Lemon Marinated Tortellini and
  Sun-dried Tomato Skewers

Mini Cherry Tomato and Basil
  Pesto Galettes

Roasted Pepper, Goat Cheese, and
  Mint Wraps

Crispy Carrot and Scallion
  Cakes with Feta and Black Olive

Herbed Artichoke and Parmesan
  Filo Rolls with Light Lemon
  Mayonnaise Dip

Focaccine Farcite with Wild
  Mushrooms and Thyme

Eggplant and Pine Nut Fritters with
  Roasted Tomato Sauce

Polenta Crostini with Blue Cheese and
  Balsamic Red Onions

•

AFTERNOON TEA MENU FOR A SUMMER WEDDING

A mix of teatime classics and contemporary inspirations - this menu sets the scene for a truly memorable occasion. Read through the THINK AHEAD *notes and begin preparation two days in advance.*

Smoked Salmon and Chive Cream
  Finger Sandwiches

Egg, Caper, and Cress Finger
  Sandwiches

Gingered Chicken Cakes with
  Cilantro Lime Mayonnaise

Tiny Parmesan and Rosemary
  Shortbreads with Roasted Cherry
  Tomatoes and Feta

Valentine Cucumber Cream Canapés

Dill Pancakes with Salmon Caviar and
  Lemon Creme Fraiche

Rare Roast Beef with Mustard
  Crème Fraîche in Poppy Seed
  Tartlets

Snow Pea Wrapped Shrimp Skewers
  with Lemon Mayonnaise

Filo Tartlets with Bang Bang Chicken

Cucumber Cups with Smoked Trout
  Mousse, Lemon, and Dill

Tiny Shortcakes with
  Strawberries and Cream

Mini Raspberry Ripple

Meringue Kisses

Notes From the Cooks on the Ingredients

ANCHOVY FILLETS If you find the flavor of anchovies too pungent, soak them in milk for 10 minutes before using.

ARUGULA Long leaves and a peppery flavor. It is very perishable. Store tightly wrapped in a plastic bag in the refrigerator for up to 2 days.

ARTICHOKE We use jars of baby globe artichoke hearts marinated in oil.

AVOCADO A **small avocado** weighs about ⅓lb (175g); a **medium avocado** weighs about ½lb (250g); a **large avocado** weighs about ¾lb (350g).

BEETS A small beet weighs about ¼lb (125g).To cook raw beets, bake, unpeeled, in a preheated 300°F (150°C) oven until tender, 1 hour.

BREADCRUMBS To make **fresh breadcrumbs**, cut bread into slices; then cut off crusts and cut into pieces. Place in a blender or food processor; pulse until finely ground. Store in an airtight container for up to 2 days.
To make **dried breadcrumbs**, cut day-old bread into slices and cut off the crusts. Bake in a preheated 300°F (150°C) oven until dry and crisp, 10 minutes. Place in a blender or food processor; pulse until finely ground. Store in an airtight container for up to 1 month.

BUCKWHEAT FLOUR Gray-brown in color with a distinct bitter flavor; available at healthfood stores and in large supermarkets.

BUTTER For this book, **butter** means unsalted or lightly salted butter.

CAPERS The pickled bud of the caper plant. We use regular and baby ones (see page 13); always drain well before using.

CARDAMOM Best used freshly ground because the fragrance diminishes with time. Open, discard the seed pods, and crush the black or brown seeds.

CAVIAR (see page 10). Salted fish roe (eggs) available in various qualities and at hugely varying prices. A little goes a long way.

CHEESE Fresh **creamy goat cheese** is a fresh, white, rindless, lightly sour cheese, available in rolls, rounds, or pyramids. As an alternative, combine 3 parts cream cheese with 1 part whole milk yogurt until smooth.
Dolcelatte cheese is a creamy, blue veined Italian cheese with a mild flavor. Use a mild blue cheese as an alternative.
Gorgonzola cheese is a rich, blueish green veined Italian cheese with a piquant flavor. Use a strong blue cheese as an alternative.
Gruyère cheese is a hard Swiss cheese with a sweet, nutty flavor. Unlike so many hard cheeses, it melts without becoming oily or rubbery. Use Emmenthal or a hard yellow cheese as an alternative.
Mascarpone cheese is a rich, velvety Italian cream cheese. As an alternative, mix 3 parts cream cheese with 1 part heavy cream and a pinch of sugar until smooth.
Parmesan cheese (see page 10) is an Italian hard cheese with a rich, sharp flavor that has nothing in common with the bland, cheesy taste of pre-grated Parmesan sold in a can. Always buy Parmesan by the piece and grate when needed.
Roquefort cheese (see page 10) is a rich, creamy, green-veined French cheese made from sheep's milk with a piquant flavor. Use a strong blue cheese as an alternative.
Stilton cheese (see page 10) is a rich, crumbly blueish green veined British cheese with a pungent flavor. Use a strong blue cheese as an alternative.

CHERVIL A very delicately flavored herb; use flat-leaf parsley as an alternative.

CHILI There are over 200 different varieties of fresh chilies, varying in color, size, shapes and heat. As a general rule, the smaller the chili the hotter it is. Capsaicin, the substance in chilies responsible for their heat, can cause a very painful burning sensation if it comes into contact with the eyes, mouth, or other sensitive skin. Make sure you wash your hands thoroughly after handling chilies, or wear rubber gloves. To reduce the level of heat remove the seeds before using.
Crushed chilies (see page 12) are a widely available hot seasoning or can be prepared at home by crushing dried chilies in a mortar and pestle or an electric coffee grinder.
Chipotles in Adobo (see page 13) are dried smoked jalapeno chilies pickled and canned in a piquant sauce made from chilies, herbs, and vinegar. Available mail order or from speciality stores.

CHILI SAUCE We use two different types; **Chinese hot chili sauce** (see page 12), made from chilies, salt, and vinegar, and **Thai sweet chili sauce** (see page 12), flavored with ginger and garlic as well as sugar, salt, vinegar, and chilies. Both available in large supermarkets or in Asian stores.

CHINESE PANCAKES Available chilled and frozen in Asian stores and large supermarkets.

CHIPOTLES IN ADOBO (see chilies).

CHORIZO Pork sausage flavored and colored with paprika frequently used in Spanish and Mexican cooking. It can be mild or highly spiced. It is mostly available cured and can be eaten without cooking.

CREME FRAICHE Thick cream with a slightly sour flavor and a velvety texture. It keeps longer than ordinary cream and can be boiled without curdling. For cooking, substitute heavy cream. For garnishing, substitute equal parts of whipped heavy cream (see page 144) combined with whole milk yogurt.

COCONUT MILK We used canned, which is available at Asian stores and large supermarkets. Shake well before opening.

CORN Available fresh on the cob or as frozen or canned kernels. To cut kernels from the cob, stand the corn upright and carefully cut downward with a sharp knife.

CORN MEAL We use yellow, medium-ground cornmeal; use Italian polenta as an alternative.

CORNICHONS Crisp pickles made from tiny gherkin cucumbers; also called cocktail gherkins.

CRAB When buying cooked crab in the shell, choose one that feels heavy for its size. Whether bought fresh, canned or frozen, cooked crabmeat should be picked over with your fingers to remove any membrane or pieces of shell.

DUMPLING WRAPPERS Small rounds of fresh noodle dough available fresh and frozen in Chinese stores or gourmet markets. They can be stored in the refrigerator for up to 1 week if well wrapped.

EGGPLANT A **medium eggplant** weighs about ⅔lb (300g).

EGGS Use large ones in our recipes; 1 beaten egg is 3 tbsp beaten egg; 1 egg yolk is 1 tbsp egg yolk; and 1 egg white is 2 tbsp egg white. **Quail eggs** (see page 11) are available at Asian markets and in the gourmet section of supermarkets. They are difficult to peel, so plunge them into cold water as soon as they are cooked and peel them under cold running water. Refrigerate them in water.

FIGS Best in season, in the late summer and early autumn months.

FISH SAUCE Thin, salty brown sauce made from fermented fish used extensively in Southeast Asian cooking. Available in large supermarkets and Asian stores. We use **Thai fish sauce** called nam pla; use light soy sauce as an alternative.

FIVE SPICE POWDER A Chinese blend of ground cloves, cinnamon, fennel, star anise, and szechuwan peppercorns.

FRUIT in all of the recipes should be washed and, unless otherwise stated, peeled.

GARLIC Unless we indicate otherwise, all garlic cloves are medium-sized.

GINGER Do not substitute ground ginger for **fresh ginger**, the flavors are quite different. Store fresh ginger wrapped in the refrigerator for up to 3 weeks. Cut off the skin with a sharp knife before measuring.
Preserved stem ginger is fresh ginger preserved in jars in a thick syrup.
Candied ginger can be substituted.
Pickled ginger (see page 12) is the Japanese condiment for sushi. It is easily recognised by its pink color, it is available in jars.

HAZELNUTS To skin hazelnuts, spread in a single layer in a baking pan and bake in a preheated 350°F/180°C oven until nutty, 10 minutes. Wrap the warm nuts in a coarse-textured dish towel and rub briskly to loosen the skin as much as possible.

HERBS Always fresh, unless otherwise specified.

HOISIN SAUCE Slightly sweet, thick, dark brown sauce made from soy beans, garlic, and spices. Keeps indefinitely in a covered jar.

LEMON CURD Best homemade. Follow the method for making passion curd (see page 127), but use ⅔ cup (150ml) lemon juice and 1tsp grated lemon peel instead of the passion fruit and lemon juice mixture.

LEMON GRASS Long, grass-like herb with a strong citrus flavor and aroma. Use only the tender inner stalk since the outer leaves are tough. It is available at Asian markets or gourmet food shops. Use a mixture of grated lime and lemon peel as an alternative.

MANGO To slice or dice a fresh mango, find where the flat side of the large seed is by rolling the mango on a work surface; it will settle on a flat side. Cut the peeled mango lengthwise on both sides of the seed so the knife just

misses it. Put each mango piece cut side down and cut it lengthwise into slices, dice if required

MASA HARINA Finely ground corn flour used to make corn tortillas; available mail order and in speciality stores.

MIRIN Japanese rice wine, sweeter than sake and used only for cooking. Use medium dry sherry as an alternative.

MUSHROOMS To clean mushrooms, be sure never to wash directly in water but, instead, wipe them with damp paper towels. **Portobello mushrooms** have an open, flat cap with exposed brown gills and a strong, savory flavor. **Shiitake mushrooms** are an Asian variety with a powerful meaty flavor. There are many varieties of **wild mushrooms**; our favorites are chanterelles, cepes (also called porcini), and morels. Field or shiitake mushrooms can be used as an alternative.

MUSTARD (see page 13). We prefer French Dijon mustard; It is available gound completely smooth or as **grainy mustard** which is made from crushed mustard seeds. **Dried mustard** is one of the strongest and hottest of mustards.

NORI Sold in paper thin sheets. It is an edible seaweed that is a popular flavoring and garnish in Japanese cooking.

ONIONS When called for in the book, an onion is a yellow onion. A **medium red onion** weighs about ¼lb (90g). A **Spanish onion** is a large, mild yellow onion. When we ask for a **scallion**, we mean both the green and white parts, unless otherwise specified. A **shallot** has a more subtle flavor than a yellow onion.

OYSTERS Ask your fish dealer to shuck the oysters for you; cover and refrigerate for up to 2 days. Smoked oysters are available in cans.

PANCETTA Flavorful Italian bacon. Store wrapped in the refrigerator for up to 3 weeks. Use regular bacon as an alternative.

PARSLEY We use flat leaf parsley in all recipes.

PASSION FRUIT Choose wrinkled passion fruit because they are riper and therefore more sweet and juicy.

PLUM SAUCE Spicy, sweet, Chinese dipping sauce made from plums, chilies, vinegar, spices, and sugar. It keeps indefinitely at room temperature in a covered jar.

POLENTA Made from ground corn, but is slightly coarser in texture and more golden in color than medium cornmeal. Use coarse cornmeal as an alternative.

POMEGRANATE Only in season during the winter months. Choose fruits with a bright yellow skin streaked with bright pink. Store in the refrigerator for up to 3 weeks.

PROSCIUTTO (see page 10) Italian raw ham that has been seasoned, salt-cured, and air-dried.

RICE PAPERS Dried brittle translucent sheets made from rice flour. Available from Asian markets, they keep indefinitely.

SAFFRON The world's most expensive spice. Choose saffron threads rather than saffron powder.

SALT Always use sea salt, whether coarse or fine.

SAKE Japan's famous rice wine is widely used as a flavoring in Japanese sauces and marinades. Use dry sherry as an alternative.

SCALLOPS Bay scallops (see page 11) are about ½ in (1cm) across. **Sea scallops** (see page 11) are larger but vary in size. For hors d'oeuvres, choose sea scallops about 2in (5cm) across.

SESAME We use Asian brands of sesame oil that are extracted from toasted sesame seeds. A lighter oil with a less intense flavor is also available in healthfood stores. Sesame seeds are widely used as a flavoring in Chinese and Japanese cooking.

SHALLOT see onion.

SHRIMP (see page 11). To devein raw shrimp, cut off the heads and peel away the shells and legs. With a sharp knife, cut along the top of each shrimp and pull out the black vein. Wash and dry well.

SOBA NOODLES Very fine Japanese buckwheat noodles (see page 156).

SOY SAUCE Major seasoning in Asian cooking and is available in a number of varieties ranging in color and flavor. We use **light soy sauce** when we want to preserve the color of the food but **dark soy sauce** imparts a richer flavor. **Japanese soy sauce** called **shoyu** is sweeter, lighter, and less salty; use light soy sauce as an alternative.

SUGAR Any white sugar (whether superfine or granulated) that you have on hand.

SUGARCANE Available fresh, frozen and canned, at Asian and Caribbean markets. When buying canned, read the label to be sure the can contains sugarcane sticks and not chopped sugarcane.

TAHINI Paste made from grinding roasted sesame seeds and sold in jars in large supermarkets and Middle Eastern markets. Shake well before using.

TOMATO For **Fresh tomatoes** we mean either round or plum and always red and ripe. Let unripe tomatoes ripen on a window sill for a few days. **Canned tomatoes** are peeled, chopped plum tomatoes. **Tomato passata** is plum tomatoes strained completely smooth and is available in cans, jars, and cartons. **Tomato paste** refers to concentrated, cooked tomatoes, available in cans or tubes. **Sundried tomatoes** are marinated in oil in jars; drain before using.

VEGETABLES Washed and, unless otherwise stated, peeled in all recipes.

VINEGAR Red wine vinegar and **white wine vinegar** have different flavors and levels of acidity and should not be used interchangeably. **Balsamic vinegar** (see page 12) is dark in color with a sweet, pungent flavor. Use red wine vinegar sweetened with a pinch of sugar as an alternative. **Rice vinegar** with its subtly sweet, mellow flavor is used extensively in Japanese cooking. White wine vinegar sweetened with a pinch of sugar can be used as an alternative in most recipes but not for flavoring sushi rice. In this case no substitution should be made.

WASABI Pungent green horseradish used in Japanese cuisine. It is available in a dried powdered form in cans and as a paste in tubes.

WHOLE MILK YOGURT Made from cow's or sheep's milk and is especially rich, creamy, and flavorful. Use thick whole milk yogurt as an alternative.

INDEX

Index compiled by Valerie Lewis Chandler

AUTHORS' ACKNOWLEDGMENTS

We would like to thank:
Three very special **Books for Cooks** cooks for their generosity and expertise. Kim Barber for her indispensible sushi masterclass and for letting us include her fabulous Sushi Rice Balls in the book. Jennifer Joyce for lending us her Southwestern and Pacific hors d'oeuvres recipes. Ursula Ferrigno for allowing us to miniaturize her Red Onion Schiaciatta and Eggplant Polpette.
Heidi Lascelles, founder and proprietor of Books for Cooks, for supporting us in all our ventures, whether writing books, teaching classes, moving house or having a baby.
Juliet Kindersley, for a mother's love, care and understanding. And for the loan of her kitchen, in which many of the recipes were tried and tested.
James Middlehurst, for giving us the green light.
Baby Frances, for letting us borrow her mummy. Her mummy Julia Pemberton Hellums for being just great, again.

And most of all, Stuart Jackman. For giving us a chance.
For making it happen.

MAIL ORDER SOURCES

DEAN AND DELUCA
560 Broadway
New York, NY 10012
800-221-7714
WWW.DEAN-DELUCA.COM
Catalogue available. Fine foods including caviar and quail's eggs and speciality ingredients from around the world.

FOODS OF INDIA
121 Lexington Avenue
New York, NY 10016
212-683-4419
Spices, dried fruit, varieties of rices and beans.

KATAGIRI
224 East 59th Street
New York, NY 10022
212-755-3566
WWW.KATAGIRI.COM
Japanese speciality ingredients.

KING ARTHUR FLOUR
P.O. Box 876
Norwich, VT 05055
800-827-6836
Baking supplies and equipment, flavorings, and many specialty ingredients.

MO-HOTTA-MO BETTA
P.O. Box 4136
San Luis Obispo, CA 93403
800-462-3220
Chilies, etc.

PENZEY'S SPICES
P.O. Box 933
Muskego, WI 53150
414-679-7207
WWW.PENZYS.COM
Wide range of spices and herbs

ZABARS
2245 Broadway
New York, NY 10024
800-697-6301
ZABARS@INFOHOUSE.COM
Fine foods.